Practical Tips for Assistants

C000149283

This book is a must have for any teaching assistant.

Confused by terminology? Difficulties in remembering the difference between CPD, CPLO, EPs and OCD? Then this is the book for you.

Teaching assistants are increasingly being asked to take on greater responsibilities within schools and this book covers all the essentials that a teaching assistant needs to know.

Presented in an easy-to-read format packed with countless suggestions, practical tips and a helpful glossary of technical terms, this is one book you will not want to be without.

Individual chapters focus on:

- What you will need to know in order to start working as a teaching assistant (TA).
- Details regarding how you will be asked to support the school.
- Strategies for supporting learning.
- Specific strategies for supporting numeracy and literacy.
- Ways of dealing with unacceptable behaviour.
- Tips for working with pupils with special needs.
- Strategies for surviving and enjoying life as a TA.

This book can be read from beginning to end or it can be used as a quick reference tool for looking up specific concerns. These concerns could include: what to do if a pupil is repeatedly calling out, how to support a pupil with visual impairments or how to look out for depression and self-harm in the pupils you support.

This book is ideal for anyone who is interested in pursuing a career as a TA, whether they are just starting to work in schools or have had more years in a classroom than they care to remember. In addition this book will be a valuable companion for students who are taking courses such as NVQ2 and 3, HLTA and foundation degrees.

Susan Bentham is presently Head of Psychology at Bognor Regis Adult Education Centre where she teaches a variety of psychology-related courses. She has many years' experience of teaching and training TAs. She is the author of two books for RoutledgeFalmer and is currently working on a third book entitled *A Teaching Assistant's Guide to Managing Behaviour in the Classroom*.

Roger Hutchins is a Special Educational Needs Coordinator (SENCO) at two primary schools.

Practical Tips for Teaching Assistants

Susan Bentham and Roger Hutchins

Routledge
Taylor & Francis Group

NEW YORK AND LONDON

First published 2006
by Routledge
2 Park Square, Milton Park, Abingdon, Oxon OX14 4RN

Simultaneously published in the USA and Canada
by Routledge
270 Madison Ave, New York, NY 10016

Routledge is an imprint of the Taylor & Francis Group

© 2006 Susan Bentham and Roger Hutchins

Typeset in Bembo by
Taylor & Francis Books
Printed and bound in Great Britain by
CPI Antony Rowe, Chippenham, Wiltshire

All rights reserved. No part of this book may be reprinted or reproduced or
utilised in any form or by any electronic, mechanical, or other means, now
known or hereafter invented, including photocopying and recording, or in
any information storage or retrieval system, without permission in writing
from the publishers.

British Library Cataloguing in Publication Data
A catalogue record for this book is available from the British Library

Library of Congress Cataloging-in-Publication Data
A catalog record for this book has been requested

ISBN10: 0–415–35472–2
ISBN13: 9-780-415-35472-2

Taylor & Francis Group is the Academic Division of T&F Informa plc.

Contents

Introduction   ix

Acknowledgements   x

1 Getting started   1

Finding your way around 1
Line managers and school hierarchies 2
Who's who in school and where they can be found 3
Your role as a TA 4
Liaison between TAs 6
Planning time for the TA and the class teacher 7
Clarifying your role 8
Playground duties 9
Coffee cups and kitchen duties 9
Contracts 10
Appraisals 11
Grievance policy 11
Mentoring and training programmes 12
Continuing professional development 12
Checklist 13

2 Supporting the school   14

Health and safety 14
Child protection 15
Looked After Children 16
Inclusion 16
Special educational needs 17
Individual Education Plans 18
Statements of educational need 19

Annual reviews 20
Record keeping 21
Assessment and marking 22
Contact with other professionals 22
Contact with parents 22
Being professional – the issue of confidentiality 23
Checklist 23

3 Strategies for enhancing learning 24

Developing a relationship with pupils 24
Questioning techniques 27
Self-esteem 29
Learning styles 31
How to use individual learning styles to support pupils 34
Teaching styles 36
How to manage your time in order to support pupils 37
How to motivate pupils 37
How to encourage independent learning 38
Supporting pupils to complete homework assignments 39
Checklist 40

4 Strategies for supporting literacy 41

The National Literacy Strategy 41
'Wave One' TA support within the literacy hour 42
'Wave Two' TA support – catch-up programmes 44
'Wave Three' TA support – intervention programmes 44
Supporting pupils who have English as an additional
* language 46*
The use of writing frames to assist pupils in writing 47
Tips for improving reading 47
Tips for improving writing 53
How to help pupils overcome spelling difficulties 55
Tips for improving handwriting 57
How to help individuals who are left-handed 58
Some words of caution 59
Checklist 59

5   Strategies for supporting numeracy 60

National Numeracy Strategy 60
Catch-up programmes 60
Difficulties presented by maths 61
Supporting pupils with special needs in maths 61
Tips for supporting numeracy 62
Checklist 65

6   Tips for dealing with unacceptable behaviour 66

The school's behaviour policy 66
The school's policy on physical restraint 66
Disclosures 68
Behaviour support plans 69
Dealing with pupils who are:
    Isolated and withdrawn 69
    Attention seeking 70
    Repeatedly calling out 71
    Over-cautious and unsure 71
    Always copying from others 72
    Defensive 73
    Immature 73
    Insecure 74
    The class clown 75
    Continuously questioning everything 76
    Limited in their attention span 77
    Taking a long time to respond 77
    Telling lies repeatedly 78
Pupils who are being bullied 78
Helping to change the behaviour of bullies 79
Restoring and rebuilding relationships with pupils 79
Checklist 80

7   Tips for TAs for supporting pupils with special needs 81

ADHD 81
Allergies 84
Asthma 85
Autistic spectrum disorder 85

Depression 88
Developmental coordination disorders/dyspraxia 89
Diabetes 91
Down's syndrome 92
Dyscalculia 94
Dyslexia 96
Epilepsy 99
Fears and phobias 99
Hearing impairments 100
Muscular dystrophy 101
Post-traumatic stress disorder 103
Self-mutilation and self-harm 103
Sexually inappropriate behaviour 104
Speech difficulties 104
Visual impairments 106
Checklist 107

8   On being a teaching assistant   108

Certainly not the money 108
How to buy a sense of humour 109
Why unions are important 109
'There's got to be something easier' 110
How to be realistic about yourself, about others and about the school 110
Stress management 112
Looking after your needs as a TA 113
Checklist 114

Appendix   115
Glossary   118
Additional resources   124
Bibliography   125
Index   129

Introduction

The aim of this book is to provide a practical hands-on reference tool for teaching assistants. We hope that there is something of value in the book for those of you who are just entering the profession as well as for those of you who have had more years of experience than you care to remember.

There are many tips within this book and at many times in it we will be cross-referencing or advising you to look at related sections. The additional resources section contains contacts that you may find useful. The glossary will help you come to grips with specialist terms, which are in bold type the first time they appear in the text. Further, the glossary will include definitions of additional, though perhaps less frequently found, special needs.

Although we have tried to include many practical and useful tips, we are all on a learning curve and these tips are not meant to be exhaustive. Those of us involved in the teaching profession are always looking out for examples of good practice. If you have any comments or suggestions, this information can be passed on to us through our publishers for incorporation into the acknowledgements in future editions of this book.

Susan Bentham

Roger Hutchins

Acknowledgements

Susan Bentham would like to thank her family for their patience and her students for their many helpful comments.

Roger Hutchins thanks his family for their support and encouragement and the staff (teachers and teaching assistants) at his schools who have provided invaluable suggestions and comments.

1 Getting started

Finding your way around – induction to the school

Ask to be shown around

Every school is different. However familiar you feel you are with the school already, there will always be something to discover.

One of the first things to do in a new post is to ask to be shown around every part of the school. Get to see everything – each classroom, every spare room, the resource area, ICT (Information and Communication Technology) area, playground, fire exits – the lot. Also, find out where the office is, where the resources are kept, where the first aid equipment is, where the fire extinguishers are. Who knows what you will need to know or what you could be asked about in the days to come?

Teaching assistants (TAs) are often regarded as the fount of all knowledge. Along with the administration staff and the caretaker, it is assumed by many that they know where anything and everything is in the school. This, of course, is often the case, but it cannot be taken for granted. It is all too easy to be taken up with the particular pupils, class or year group with which you will be working, so it is useful to gain the 'big picture' of the school early on in your career.

Find out about relevant resources

Of special importance in the induction process are the resources you can use when working with pupils. You need to be shown what resources are available, what they are to be used for, how they are to be used and where they are kept. Resources for children are to be seen as a toolkit, with specific tools being used for specific jobs, but if you are unaware of them, you will not be able to choose the most appropriate tools. There is nothing more frustrating than preparing loads of resources for a particular pupil or group of pupils, only to find out later that those resources already existed. Beware of reinventing the wheel.

The induction process

Ideally, an induction process should take place within the first week or two of taking on the job. Starting right reduces pressures and tensions. A thorough induction to the school, although it takes time, contributes to maintaining sanity.

An induction process in school should involve a meeting with the **Special Educational Needs Coordinator (SENCO)** about **special educational needs (SEN)** in the school in general. Many TAs find it helpful to know something about the background to the work they are going to do. This gives a sense of perspective and reason to it all. Do not, however, expect to remember everything you get told. There is too much to take in, in one go.

You should be shown the **Special Educational Needs Code of Practice** (Department for Education and Employment (DfEE), 2001). You should also be told about **Individual Education Plans (IEPs)** (see pages 18–19, 46, 69): how they are written, what use is made of them in school, how often they are reviewed and who is involved in that review process.

Induction is important because, once you are full-swing in your job, it is all too easy to assume knowledge. Remember, assumption is the mother of all foul-ups.

'Who's my boss?' – line managers and school hierarchies

Every school is different in its organisation and hierarchies. Part of the induction should include how your particular school operates. There are, however, some general principles to which every school should adhere.

Board of governors

Legally speaking, the group of people with ultimate responsibility for what happens in the school is the board of governors. These are volunteers who oversee every aspect of school life and act as 'critical friends' to the school.

Who is the line manager for the TA?

Ultimately this is the head teacher. The Code of Practice describes the head teacher as having responsibility for the overall management of special needs, and this includes staff employed to help meet those needs. Working with the head teacher is the school's SENCO, who has responsibility for the day-to-day 'operation' of the special needs provision in the school. The line manager for TAs is therefore likely to be the SENCO. Within secondary schools a number of people may share this role, such as heads of year or heads of departments. TAs in these situations are organised to support pupils either within year groups or within subject areas.

However, TAs usually work in classes, and, within the class, the class teacher has the responsibility for what happens. Day to day, then, the immediate managers of the TAs are the class teachers within whose classes they work.

Communication is the key

Are you confused yet? If you are, you are in good company. The potential for confusion exists in every school. You can easily find yourself being told three different things by three different people, all of whom have good ideas and have both the interests of the pupils and your interests at heart. The end result may be that you do not know whether you should be doing spelling, reading, handwriting or flying to the moon with the group of children you have been asked to work with for the next half-hour.

The answer is – it's all down to teamwork. No one person or even group of people can make a school function smoothly and provide an environment where each child can learn. It is everybody mucking in together, talking to one another, sharing ideas and resolving issues.

One key is communication. Another key is having a good attitude. Nobody is perfect. No system is perfect. Problems will inevitably arise. A *problem-solving* rather than a *problem-raising* mentality is crucial to a well-functioning school.

However, if you do find yourself in the midst of confusion, or even conflict, you must not sit on it, trying to work it out yourself. Talk to someone about it – the class teacher, the SENCO, the head teacher, other TAs.

Who has responsibility for TAs and for what they do is a whole-school issue, and one which must be addressed by the whole school under the leadership of the senior management and the head teacher.

Personnel list – who's who in school and where they can be found

Ask for a copy of the staff handbook

When you start work, ask for a list of personnel in the school. It is worth finding out not only the names of every staff member in the school, but also their roles and responsibilities. Many schools produce a staff handbook, which is an excellent means of communicating simply and efficiently 'who's who' in the school.

You need to know who is the staff member through whom contacts with external agencies are made. This will usually be the head teacher, deputy head or the SENCO – or any combination of the three.

You need to know all this because one day you might need to talk to them about pupils with whom you are working. Although your first port of call will always be the class teacher, it is important for you to be able to discuss areas of concern or to ask questions of those members of staff with specific responsibilities for particular areas.

The personnel list should include information about who knows about reprographic equipment and ICT in the school. Different schools employ different procedures for the use of photocopiers, laminators, digital cameras and the like. As you are likely to be asked to photocopy resources, find out how your school operates before you either make too much work for yourself or find yourself treading on somebody else's toes.

It is also worth finding out about the roles of the administration staff. Which person, for instance, deals with dinner money, which with first aid and accidents, which with letters home, and so on? At some stage you may be asked to deal with this sort of thing, and you need to know where to go for help.

If you want to use a computer with an individual child and there is something wrong with it, to whom do you go? If you have found this out beforehand, it saves a bit of stress.

All this is designed to make your job easier. It may be a lot of information to take onboard all in one go, which is why having things written down helps. You do not have to remember everything if you have policies and procedures to hand to which you can refer.

'All pencil sharpening and cleaning paint brushes?' – your role as a TA

Ask for a job description

Much confusion can be saved by referral to an accurate and current job description. It should be part of the professional status of TAs. If there is no clear job description, things can get hazy and, again, assumptions can lead to misunderstandings and even conflict.

In many people's minds there is still the sense that TAs are little more than a 'mum's army', present in the classroom to sharpen pencils and clean paint brushes. Whilst this may be what you do sometimes (after all, in certain year groups both are needful occupations), it is not the sum total of your responsibilities.

As a TA, you are a professional member of a professional team. Together with the class teacher, you are there to create an environment where children learn and develop to their fullest potential. Stephanie Lorenz describes the TA as a 'Bridge-Builder' between the pupil and the curriculum (Lorenz, 2002, p. 96). You are not there simply to do practical things to keep the classroom ticking over whilst the class teacher gets on with the real job.

By definition, and certainly by practice, TAs teach. They may not necessarily teach the whole class and they certainly do not have the responsibility to decide what should be taught or how it should be taught. But TAs share with the class teacher the delivery of the curriculum to the children in their care.

Find out what is expected of you

The job description should specify the role of the TA in quite some detail. '*Generally helping in the classroom*' is not a good description of what is expected of a TA. If the job description you have been given reads something like that, question it. Ask what will be specifically required of you.

Many schools specify the role of TAs in their SEN or inclusion policies along these sorts of lines: TAs will effectively support children by:

- Explaining and clarifying instructions.
- Motivating and encouraging the children.
- Ensuring children have access to and are able to use materials needed to complete tasks.
- Meeting any necessary physical needs (e.g. checking hearing aids) whilst promoting independence.
- Establishing caring and supportive relationships with the children.
- Developing methods of promoting children's self-esteem.
- Encouraging pupils' participation in their own assessment and target setting.
- Assisting in the delivery of the curriculum and specific programmes of study.
- Teaching individuals and/or small groups as appropriate.

Teaching assistants are an essential part of education today. Most agree that without them, the national agenda of **inclusion** would not happen. Whilst this remains to be reflected in conditions of service, pay and career structure, TAs are increasingly being recognised as a profession in their own right. They are not 'budding teachers', although many might be very capable as teachers and may want to pursue this as a career. They are certainly not a 'mum's army'. They are TAs with a role and a professionalism which are theirs alone.

Liaison between TAs

Find out about mentoring systems

One of your most important sources of information will be the other TAs. Some schools operate a 'mentoring' system whereby newly appointed TAs are nurtured in their new roles by a more experienced TA. Whether there is an official mentoring system in place or not, ask other TAs regarding anything you are unsure about.

Many TAs are asked to work with specific children using particular programmes of support. At first sight, these programmes may appear quite daunting. Often other TAs who have used them in the past or are currently using them are the best people to help you. It is most helpful not only to talk about the programme with someone experienced in its use, but also to watch them in action.

'Job shadowing' in this way during the first week or so of being appointed to the post can be one of the easiest and most profitable sources of training for the new TA. Remember, everybody started the same way. All had to learn somehow and most learning takes place 'on the job'.

The value of team meetings

Many schools hold regular meetings between the SENCO and TAs. Although this cuts into the school day, such team meetings can be a useful forum for liaison between TAs. The meetings should certainly be more than an opportunity for giving out notices. Team meetings provide an opportunity for sharing concerns and successes. New programmes can be introduced. TAs familiar with certain programmes can show them to the others. Specific programmes can be placed in the context of whole-school learning. It is very important for each TA to see how they 'fit' into the larger scheme of things.

Team meetings can also be an opportunity for TAs to discuss situations they are finding difficult. This is not at all the same thing as a general moaning session. It is rather a space in the school week to seek to solve problems together. But, before problems can be solved, they must be aired. It is often the case that what one TA is finding difficult, others are too, and by raising it the TA no longer feels isolated.

'On a wing and a prayer' – planning time for the TA and the class teacher

Find out about planning time

Most educationalists recognise the need for adequate planning time between TAs and class teachers so that they can work together effectively as a partnership. They can consider how to adapt resources to meet the needs of particular children and agree how each of them will support those pupils. This time is also useful for reviewing existing provision, particularly with regard to assessing the effectiveness of any intervention strategies being employed (see page 43).

However, a common complaint heard from both TAs and teachers alike is the little time available to plan and talk through issues together. Often any discussion between teachers and TAs has to be snatched between lessons or at break times. In many schools it really is a matter of 'on a wing or a prayer', or, alternatively, 'flying by the seat of your pants'. For TAs, not knowing what is coming up in a lesson, and especially not knowing beforehand what they will be expected to do, can be stressful. 'On a wing and a prayer' can be exciting for persons of a certain disposition, but for most of us it is disconcerting. This pressure can be especially difficult in secondary schools, where both teachers and TAs are hurrying from one lesson to another with little or no time to discuss pupils or planning beforehand.

One reason why planning time is at such a premium is the fact that TAs are commonly paid only for contact time with the children. This means that any planning outside of that is in their own time. As they get paid so little, such extra work should not be expected of them. Paying TAs extra or seeking to alter their timetable to allow for meetings out of school hours can be difficult as very many TAs have young families and need to be with their children.

Another reason for the lack of time given to planning is the pace of life within the school week. Once Monday morning begins with children flooding through the school gate, it can often seem that there is continuous motion with no time to stop and think until the school gate closes on a Friday afternoon. Within the normal school day there simply isn't the opportunity to talk together in any meaningful way unless it is definitely booked in.

It is well worth finding out how contact is 'unofficially' maintained between the TA and teacher. Ask the TAs already employed in the school – they are the ones with the information. You need to know whether, despite what is officially documented in the school, there is an expectation that TAs attend staff meetings or lunchtime Key Stage meetings, or whether they are on the phone with teachers of an evening. If that is the expectation and, indeed, the precedent set by previous TAs, you need to decide whether you are happy with that before you take on the job.

You need to know how teachers communicate with TAs regarding what they expect from them in lessons. It may be that teachers pin up planning sheets on the classroom wall at the start of each week. Providing this planning clearly identifies the support to be given by the TA, this can be very useful. It may be that there is a daily contact book in use, in which teachers write what they want the TA to do for that day. In secondary schools, it may be more a case of snatching a quick conversation before class or in the staff room. Whatever the case, as a new TA you need to be made aware of what procedures are in place so that you can support the pupils and support the teacher as fully as possible from the word go.

Clarifying your role

'What tensions could you see occurring within your role, and how would you go about resolving them?'

Tensions can and do arise between TA and class teacher when there is not an agreed perspective on the relative roles and responsibilities of the two. This can be particularly the case when, for whatever reason, TAs find themselves working with a number of teachers. Perhaps there are a string of supply teachers in the class or the particular pupil a TA is working with is actually being taught by two or three different teachers. This is more likely to be the case in secondary schools, but can also occur in primary schools.

It is, in the first instance, the responsibility of the head teacher and the senior management of the school to ensure that all staff (class teachers and TAs) 'sign up' to the same understanding of their respective roles. Although there may well be a written policy on this, in reality much of this is developed over time through practice.

A teacher newly appointed to the school, or a supply teacher unfamiliar with the ethos of the school, needs to be made aware of the role of the extra adult (or adults) in the class. But this may not happen. With the best will in the world, such clarification may get overlooked. If that does happen, it is worth the TAs' clarifying teacher expectations for themselves. For instance, does the class teacher want the TA to help with discipline in the classroom, or is the teacher happy for the TA to mark books, give permission for children to change reading books, go to the toilet, start a new piece of work, speak with parents? Do not assume that one teacher will view the role of the TA in the same way as another one. Always seek to clarify expectations before any situation arises.

This can be daunting for both TA and teacher. On the other hand, it can be a great strength. A new teacher to the class may be very grateful for suggestions from an experienced TA who knows both the children and the routines of the school. But always remember to phrase your suggestions positively – treat others as you would like others to treat you.

Playground duties

Know playground procedures

In many schools TAs are asked to undertake playground duty. This can be a further source of tension if some TAs do this and others do not, but they all get paid the same. Again, the answer is communication and clarification. This should be made clear in the job description.

If you know you are going to be on playground duty, find out beforehand the procedures the children should follow both during and at the end of play. These are often decided at staff meetings where TAs are not normally present and are not necessarily communicated to other members of staff. It can easily be assumed that everyone simply 'knows what to do', and they do not.

Anyone who has been in education for more than a few weeks will readily agree that tensions between children arise at playtimes more than during lessons, so knowing what to do if you are on duty is vital. During break times accidents happen. You need to know who to call for and what to do to record it. You need to know your responsibilities and you need to know when to call for somebody else.

During break times arguments break out, usually over whether it was a goal or not, or whether that handball should be a penalty. Given that most TAs are not professional football referees, these arguments can blow up quickly, are hard to resolve and can easily spill over into class as the children go back to their lessons. You need to know what your responsibility is as the person on duty to help resolve such arguments and when you are to leave it up to the class teacher or somebody else to sort out.

What do you do if a fight breaks out between pupils? Find out before it happens. It is too late when little Johnny has just given little Freddy a bleeding nose.

Coffee cups and kitchen duties

Who cleans up?

Whatever officialdom says, schools are run on caffeine and cakes – everyone knows this. But who does the clearing up?

Teachers are amazingly messy animals. Staff rooms at the end of a normal working day often bear more than a passing resemblance to a bomb site. Alongside the latest edition of the *Times Educational Supplement*, missals from the LEA (Local Education Authority) or government and school policies being debated and decided upon, there are piles of dirty coffee cups and plates.

Many staff rooms have now entered the twenty-first century and dishwashers are plumbed in, but, as seems to be the case at home, loading the dishwasher is one thing, unloading it is another. All too easily there can be an assumption that TAs will clean up the staff room.

This is, or should be, a false assumption. Part of the essence of teamwork is that each member of the team shoulders responsibility for communal areas, including staff rooms. Again, the key is communication and organisation. If you are not sure what the procedure is in your school, ask. It may seem a trivial matter compared to some of the challenges facing education today, but woe betide the staff room at the beginning of break or lunch when teachers and TAs alike descend upon it only to discover that there are no clean cups.

Contracts

Ensure you have a written contract

Every TA should have a written contract with the school or the LEA. Given that, in the end, everything is determined by funding, contracts vary for TAs from permanent contracts to temporary ones, sometimes covering only a few months at a time.

Whilst permanent contracts tie the school down more than temporary contracts, for the TA they provide job security. However, we continue to live in an age where some, if not most, funding is linked to specific pupils, and when those pupils leave the school, the funding leaves with them. Where that is the case, it is difficult for schools always to provide permanent contracts. Similarly, if a school cannot guarantee a certain level of funding year on year for TAs, then it is unable to offer permanent contracts to all.

Whatever the case, it is important that, right from the beginning – indeed, from before you agree to take the job on – you know what sort of contract you are being offered. Check particularly the hours you will be expected to work. This is especially important if you are being employed on a part-time basis. Ensure you have in writing the actual hours you are to work in the school. This is to clarify expectations so that no misunderstandings and confusions arise in the future.

Part of the contract should stipulate rates of pay, and whether payment is being made for break times and lunchtimes. Schools differ in what they offer. Always check it out.

Volunteer staff will not have contracts, but there are certain expectations and commitments from both the person and the school which should be agreed and made explicit before any work begins.

Appraisals

Find out about appraisals

As part of the process of developing the role of TAs as a profession in their own right, schools, encouraged by government initiatives and communications, are including TAs in the process of appraisal (DfEE, 2000).

An appraisal is designed to be a regular (usually annual) opportunity for an employee to meet with their line manager on an individual basis to look back over the year, celebrate what has gone well, identify areas that could be strengthened, set targets for the coming year and agree together how those targets can be met. An appraisal is certainly not supposed to be a place where the line manager assesses or criticises the employee. Nor is an appraisal the place where the employee merely pours out a whole load of complaints.

In other words, appraisals, although time consuming, are designed to be of benefit to all.

For TAs, the person most likely to be conducting and organising appraisals is the SENCO. In order for appraisals to be useful and thorough, there needs to be three parts to the process. The SENCO needs to observe the TA in action. The SENCO needs to talk with the class teacher(s) about how the TA is functioning in class. Most importantly, the SENCO and TA need to talk together following a structured pattern which will include an overview of the past year and setting targets for the year to come, along with an outline of the means to achieve those targets.

Grievance policy

What happens if things go wrong?

Of course, we all hope they don't and, usually, things run smoothly. However, there can, for all sorts of reasons, be occasions when some kind of breakdown in operations occurs.

It is helpful if the school has a written grievance policy or complaints procedure, which sets out the steps to be followed in such instances. If you do have a grievance, ensure you follow the procedures in the policy (see page 110).

Depending on what your grievance is about, your first port of call is likely to be either the class teacher with whom you are working or the

SENCO. It is the job of the senior management of the school to ensure that all employees are treated equally and fairly, so recourse to the deputy head or head teacher should also be available. If you get no satisfaction from any of these sources, the governing body, and in particular the SEN governor and/or the Grievance Committee of the governors, are there to discuss matters with you. Finally, if you are working in a maintained school, you are likely to be employed by the LEA itself and you can talk to the personnel department there.

When thinking about things going wrong, it is worth seriously thinking about joining a trade union. Several unions represent TAs, but the largest currently is UNISON. Trade unions are dealt with in more detail in a later chapter (see page 109).

Mentoring and training programmes

Find out about mentoring schemes

Newly qualified teachers (NQTs) have other teachers to act as mentors during their first year of teaching. The government recommends that TAs also have mentors (DfEE, 2000).

Every LEA is supposed to provide at least one induction course for new TAs each year. This is a government-sponsored course, lasting four or five days. The government provides the resources, the LEA provides the trainers and the schools provide the mentors.

Whether you attend such a training course or not, if this is your first time in the job, it will be very helpful to have a mentor, someone clearly designated to support you, introduce you to the school and to education in general, and someone to whom you can turn throughout your first year for advice and help. Usually, but not necessarily, this will be the SENCO. It could equally be a more experienced TA. Find out what mentoring procedures and initial training programmes are offered by the school.

Continuing professional development

Find out information regarding continuing professional development

Continuing professional development (CPD) is emphasised for all members of staff, teachers and TAs alike. LEAs, colleges of further education, universities and voluntary organisations provide numerous courses each year. Training available ranges from half-day courses on something specific to five-year degree courses in learning support. As part of your induction you should be told where you can find information regarding these courses and what the procedures are for applying to attend them. You should also be told about funding arrangements.

Schools have a responsibility to ensure that TAs as well as teachers are given the opportunity to develop their professional expertise. One member of staff should be responsible for CPD. Find out who this is and talk to this person and to the SENCO about what would be most suitable for you.

Checklist

✓ A thorough induction programme is essential for a good start in school.
✓ A 'problem-solving' mentality is crucial.
✓ Make sure you have been given a current and relevant job description.
✓ Liaising with other TAs and teachers can be extremely helpful.
✓ Clarity is needed over your role in class, your duties outside of the classroom and your contract.
✓ Continuing professional development should be available to you.

2   Supporting the school

Health and safety

Be familiar with the policies

The first concern of any school and any member of staff is to ensure that, at all times, children are safe. As a TA, therefore, whatever else you do, you need to look after the physical and mental well-being of the pupils with whom you come into contact.

Under no circumstances should any member of staff physically hit or verbally abuse any pupil (see page 68). Corporal punishment has been outlawed in British schools for many years, but psychological punishment can also be damaging. There is no place for sarcasm or criticism of children themselves.

The Race Relations Amendment Act (2001) places a legal obligation on all school staff actively to promote racial understanding and harmony. To fulfil your obligations under this legislation, at the very least you need to know the procedure for reporting racial incidents. The school's Race Relations Policy, which may be subsumed within the Equal Opportunities Policy, will give you this information. You need to familiarise yourself with both policies.

A school's duty of care is reflected in every staff member treating every pupil, and every other member of staff, with respect and dignity. There is no place for bullying, not only between pupils but between members of staff and between adults and pupils (see page 78).

The school nurse

Each school has a nurse attached to it. If you are working with children who have health issues you may well need to meet with the nurse to discuss any issues arising or to receive training. Whilst no member of staff is required to administer medication, some should be available to do so, and this may well include TAs (see page 85). You will need to receive training, therefore, on such procedures as the use of Epi-pens or the correct way to respond to a seizure (see page 99).

Child protection

Become familiar with policy and procedures

By law, every school must have a Child Protection Policy. Be sure that you are familiar with this and that you know who the school's **Child Protection Liaison Officer (CPLO)** is. It can often be the case that the first adult to raise concerns about a pupil's well-being is the TA who works closely with them. The TA may observe what teachers do not have the opportunity to see. The TA may also be the one to whom a child turns if they are in difficulty. It may be that when you are working with a child they will disclose information to you which leads you to suspect the need for some kind of child protection. If that happens, you need to know what to do, and the Child Protection Policy should tell you (see page 66).

Signs of abuse and/or neglect include:

- Physical marks (cuts, bruises, etc.) beyond what would normally be expected for children.
- Sudden or prolonged change in behaviour, e.g. aggression or withdrawal, which is out of character for the child.
- Personal hygiene issues, e.g. persistent dirty clothes, children unwashed, regular incidents of soiling.
- Language, terminology and subject matter used by the child in conversation, e.g. overtly sexual at a level of understanding beyond what is normal.
- Actual disclosure by the child to an adult (or to other children and reported to an adult).

Procedures regarding disclosures

The Children Act (1989) guides school procedures, and the principles apply to all situations. If you receive information about abuse from a child, you will need to display sensitivity and tact in responding to the disclosure. You will need to retain the trust of the child whilst also explaining the need for action, which may necessitate the involvement of other adults. You should listen carefully and record accurately in the language used by the child, at the earliest opportunity. You must not offer alternative explanations for the child's concerns or ask leading questions. As soon as you can, you must report your concerns to the school's CPLO and they will take the matter forward (see pages 68, 69, 139, 164).

You have a legal duty to report any concerns and suspicions. It is not your responsibility to make a judgement as to whether the child is telling the truth or not, nor whether the matter is serious enough to warrant taking further.

Looked After Children

Who are 'Looked After Children'?

National legislation identifies groups of 'vulnerable pupils' and one such group are those who are looked after by the local authority. The local authority acts as corporate parents for such children. Most children 'in care' live in foster homes, with around 10 per cent in children's homes. A further 10 per cent live with their own families, whilst remaining looked after by the local authority.

Children who are 'looked after' are statistically much more likely than any other identifiable group of children to experience disrupted education, to leave school with little or no formal qualifications, to have **Statements of Educational Need**, to truant or to be permanently excluded from school. They may well exhibit challenging behaviours in school as they seek to come to terms with a level of loss and turbulence unknown to other children (see pages 46, 74, 103).

Refer to the Looked After Link Teacher

Schools have an important part to play in meeting the needs of these children, and you as a TA may be asked specifically to support Looked After Children. You should not ask them why they are in care. This can be a cause of distress to children. If, however, they choose to talk about it with you, then that is another matter. Within the school, you can expect to receive advice and support from the **Looked After Link Teacher (LALT)**. You need to know who this is as the LALT has the responsibility to oversee the needs of Looked After Children and act as an advocate for them.

Inclusion

What is inclusion?

All schools are now operating within the national and international inclusion agenda. One aim of government is that no person or group of persons should be discriminated against on the basis of gender, race or ability/

disability. This is not to say that everyone should be treated in exactly the same way by attempting to sweep all differences under the carpet. In fact, the opposite is true. An inclusive education system is one which celebrates diversity, recognises differences and seeks to meet the needs of all in an appropriate and meaningful way.

It would be foolish to say that all society's ills can be solved by schools, but schools can and do have a profound influence on the way children and young people grow up. The aim of inclusive education is to promote understanding and tolerance so that an inclusive rather than a divisive or exclusive society is created. To this end, the assumption now is that all pupils will attend mainstream schools unless there is a good reason why they should not, and that those schools will adapt their provision to meet the needs of those pupils. In most LEAs there remains a role for special schools, but there is no longer the automatic assumption that a child with complex difficulties will attend them.

The role of the TA in the inclusion process

School staff conduct their work against this backdrop of inclusion, but the actual impact of inclusive education varies between schools. For some the principle remains just that, a principle; but for others, inclusion is a way of life. Central to the inclusion process are the TAs. It is generally agreed that without TAs, inclusion cannot happen.

The reason is simple. Many pupils now attending mainstream schools require significant levels of additional adult support. Not every pupil coming to mainstream school with some measure of disability or learning difficulty will require such support, but many will, and it is the TAs who provide this support.

Special educational needs (SEN)

The SEN Code of Practice (DfEE, 2001)

One of the main purposes of the Code of Practice, often referred to as the CoP, is to ensure that identification of and provision for special educational needs is consistent throughout the country. Be sure you get to see a copy of this document; it is the single most important government publication regarding SEN.

The CoP was distributed to schools in a purple and white box called the *SEN Toolkit*, which also contained a range of booklets and a government publication on inclusive schooling. The booklets outline and summarise the main principles and points of the CoP and make relatively easy reading. It is important to be familiar with the contents of this toolkit because this is probably going to be the sphere within which you will work.

The staged approach

There is no distinct 'cut-off' between children with SEN and those without. Every school should have in place stages relating to degrees of provision. The CoP describes these stages as Early Identification (EI), School Action (SA) and School Action Plus (SA+), with slightly different terminology being used for the Early Years.

Early Identification is the most basic level of intervention and occurs when a class teacher identifies a child as experiencing a measure of difficulty in school. Intervention at this stage is organised by the class teacher within the class using resources generally available.

At *School Action* the class teacher identifies a pupil experiencing SEN and devises interventions *additional to* or *different from* those provided as part of the school's usual curriculum. The class teacher and SENCO are jointly responsible for drawing up a programme of intervention. They will write an Individual Education Plan (IEP) which specifies targets for that pupil and outlines what provision will be put in place to meet those targets.

The highest level of intervention within a school is *School Action Plus*, when the school, in consultation with parents, asks for help from external services such as **educational psychologists (EPs)**.

Role of TAs

TAs would normally be expected to work alongside pupils who are at School Action or above. Their role is usually part of the provision outlined for these pupils on their IEPs. If this is the case, each child you work with should have an up-to-date IEP.

Individual Education Plans (IEPs)

What is an IEP?

An IEP is a working document which is intended to draw together planning, teaching techniques and reviewing procedures for individual pupils into one place. It should set out *what* is to be taught and *how* it is to be taught. The essential aspect of the IEP is that it focuses on activities which are *additional to* or *different from* those provided for all pupils through the normal class curriculum. IEPs must be accessible and understandable to all concerned (see pages 2, 69).

IEP targets

IEPs should focus on up to three or four individual short-term targets and should include information about:

- The teaching strategies to be used.
- The provision to be put in place.
- When the plan is to be reviewed.
- Success criteria, specifying how staff and pupils will know when the targets have been met.
- Outcomes (to be recorded when the IEP is reviewed).

All IEP targets must be *achievable* for both the pupil and the teacher. To be valid, pupils must know what the targets are and agree to work towards them, otherwise they can become little more than a wish-list.

TAs and IEPs

Very often it will be the TA who actually implements the IEP, so it is important to find out the process used by the school in drawing up, using and reviewing IEPs. You need to know to what extent you as a TA are expected to be involved in reviewing the IEP, in assessing to what extent targets have been met, in discussing and agreeing appropriate provision to meet those targets.

You need to know who is responsible for actually writing the IEPs. Normally, it will be either the SENCO or class/subject teachers in discussion with each other.

You also need to know where the IEPs are kept. As they are confidential documents, they should be in a reasonably secure place; but, as you need the IEP to develop and plan your support for the pupil, you need to have access to it. One useful way is for you to have your own file in which you can keep all your records and plans as well as the IEPs.

Statements of Educational Need

What are statements?

If a child's needs are so severe or complex that provision at School Action or School Action Plus will not be sufficient, or if a child has been supported at those stages and has still made little or no progress over a period of time, then consideration may be given to providing that child with a *Statement of Educational Need*.

A statement is a legal document which sets out the needs of a child and the provision to be made for that child by an LEA. There is a good deal of controversy regarding statements, with some feeling they are little more than a bureaucratic burden whilst others see them as essential to providing adequate education for children with complex needs.

The layout of a statement

There are six parts to a statement. Following an Introduction, Part Two sets out the nature and severity of the child's difficulties and the implications of these difficulties for the child. Part Three specifies the provision to be made by the LEA and the school to meet the child's special needs. It sets out the main long-term objectives to be achieved by this provision, such as 'develop basic literacy and numeracy skills' or 'access the **National Curriculum** at an appropriate level'. Included in the provision, the statement identifies any facilities and equipment which are needed and sets out any staffing arrangements and curriculum modifications which are to be made.

When a statement is initially drawn up (known as a 'Provisional Statement'), Part Four is left blank so that parents can state their preferred school. In the Final Statement, Part Four specifies the type of school and the name of the particular school which is considered appropriate for the child.

Part Five identifies any non-educational needs of the child and Part Six specifies the non-educational provision which is required to meet the needs identified in Part Five.

Annual reviews

What are annual reviews?

Monitoring the effectiveness and the relevance of a statement takes place at least once a year via an annual review. This is a legally prescribed meeting of all involved in the education of the pupil, including parents, LEA representatives, school staff and external agencies. Annual reviews are organised by the head teacher or SENCO.

All parties, including the pupils themselves, are given the opportunity to comment on the progress being made by the pupil and the effectiveness of the provision for that pupil. Each contributes towards the setting of new targets and the provision to be put in place over the next year in order to meet those targets.

Following the meeting a report is drawn up which is circulated to all those invited to the meeting. This report is considered by the LEA who decide on whether to maintain the statement as it is, amend it, draw up a new statement or cease it altogether.

If you are a TA working with a child who has a statement, you may well be required to attend and contribute to annual reviews by providing information on the progress of the pupil and the suitability of interventions and by giving suggestions regarding future objectives.

Record keeping

Know the process for record keeping

You need to keep accurate records regarding the pupils with whom you are working. Each school is going to have its own system for recording progress, but whatever the precise system, some principles apply to all:

- Always date and sign records. Remember, they are there for others to read and they need to know whether what you have written applies to the child last week or last year.
- Be precise. You do not need to go into detail about everything the pupil did when they were with you. Nobody is going to want to wade through three pages of close-typed print to find out whether a pupil has learnt to spell 'what'.
- Give enough information. You need to give somebody else an understanding as to how the pupil is progressing. It is not sufficient, therefore, to write something like 'a good lesson' and leave it at that. Records should contain objective information, not value judgements. Something like '[Name] has been able to spell 10 cvc words in his test and can now read the first 20 of the high frequency words' is far more useful.
- Make records regarding progress towards specific targets.
- Comment on the suitability of the provision being made for the pupil. Lack of progress may well be down to the fact that pupils are being asked to do something which is too hard, too easy or simply inappropriate. Your records should indicate any concerns you have about this.

Time should be allocated to you to complete all necessary records. If it has not been, discuss this with the teacher or SENCO. You need to be shown where to keep records and they need to be shared with the teacher and, when needed, with the SENCO. Your records are likely to be essential documents when reviewing IEPs or preparing for annual reviews, so they need to be accurate, reliable and up-to-date.

Assessment and marking

Become familiar with marking policies

Schools differ regarding how TAs are involved in marking and assessment. If, in your school, you are asked to mark pupils' work, make sure you are familiar with that school's marking policy and that you mark in accordance with the policy.

When marking pupils' work, you need not only to know how you are to mark, but also to know why you are marking. '**Assessment for learning**' is something many schools are developing and seeks to train staff to mark so that children can learn from that marking by setting targets for themselves. If you are to be involved in such a process, you, too, will need to receive training.

Contact with other professionals

The role of the TA

If you are working with pupils at School Action Plus or who have a statement, you are likely to encounter professionals from external agencies such as educational psychologists, **occupational therapists** or **speech and language therapists**. Depending on the level of support you are giving to the pupil and depending on the set-up within the school, you may actually be the main point of contact for such agencies.

This can be a great advantage as you get to discuss at first hand matters that concern you on a daily basis. The disadvantage is that the teacher, who is the one responsible for the education of all pupils within the class, could get missed out of the loop. As in most things to do with school, the key is communication.

If you are not involved in face-to-face liaison with external agencies, you need to see the reports they write about the pupils with whom you are working. Such reports contain the results of any assessments or observations they have made and make recommendations regarding future support.

Contact with parents

Be familiar with policies and procedures regarding contact with parents

One of the key principles of the SEN CoP is partnership with parents. Almost certainly, therefore, you will have direct contact with parents. Parents are involved at annual reviews, IEP reviews, particularly for pupils at School Action Plus, and meetings with external agencies. Where there are issues of concern over behaviour, parents are likely to be involved in meetings with teachers and, possibly, senior management. TAs may be involved in any or all of such meetings. There may be a school policy regarding contact with parents. Make sure you are aware of this. As in all things, if in doubt, check it out.

Being professional – the issue of confidentiality

Confidentiality is a crucial issue, and one that cannot be taken for granted. Whilst schools are not closed, secret organisations where every piece of information is classified, there will be aspects of school life which can be quite sensitive. As employees in the school, TAs are likely to know about pupil progress, difficulties encountered by specific pupils, possibly even issues of child protection. As a TA it is your duty and responsibility to be professional and respect the confidentiality of pupils and staff alike.

Parental contact should be approached with exactly the same level of professionalism as contact with any other person. You are working with pupils as an employee of the school and you need to be careful how you talk about your work. It is always better to say too little than too much.

Checklist

✓ Health and safety are overriding concerns within a school.
✓ Become familiar with issues relating to child protection and Looked After Children.
✓ Inclusion is the agenda to which all schools are working.
✓ Special educational needs (SEN) lie at the core of what many TAs do.
✓ SEN are guided by the *Special Educational Needs Code of Practice*.
✓ Individual Education Plans (IEPs) are central documents within SEN.
✓ Special needs provision is graded from *Early Intervention* to *Statements of Educational Need*.
✓ Accurate record keeping is an essential aspect of the job.
✓ Assessment and marking may also be part of your role.
✓ You might be involved in liaison with agencies from outside the school.
✓ Confidentiality is crucial.

3   Strategies for enhancing learning

TAs will often say that their reason for being in the classroom is to help pupils to learn. Some pupils find learning easy, while others struggle. Some pupils will immediately understand new concepts, be these concepts basic addition or the use of metaphors in *Hamlet*. But what of the pupils who still do not understand even after numerous explanations? What do you say to the pupil who still thinks that 2 + 2 = 5? It is the pupils who struggle that will need your support. This chapter will look at various strategies that will enable you to support pupils more effectively.

Developing a relationship with pupils

Make the relationship positive

A positive working relationship with pupils is central to the role of a TA. A positive working relationship is characterised by open and honest communication, being able to handle dialogue in a constructive manner and consistent and effective support – something called **constructive feedback**. As a TA you will strive to be open and honest with the pupils you support and hope that they are open and honest with you. However, what if you have to tell pupils off? What if one of your pupils has answered every question on the worksheet incorrectly? On the other hand what if the pupils get really angry with you or tell you that it is your fault that they don't understand? This is where handling dialogue in a constructive manner is essential. Part of your role involves learning how to say the 'difficult things' but in a way that the pupils can accept and learn from. For example, rather than saying 'the question is incorrect' you could say 'shall we look at this together?'

The final aspect of a positive working relationship is consistent and effective support. The relationship you have with pupils is ongoing and will take time to develop. It is important that you are seen to be treating all pupils equally and fairly at all times. However, as a TA you need to be gentle with yourself. Do not expect that the pupils will immediately respond to you or that you will magically know the right thing to say. What is important is that you are committed to supporting the pupils you work with. If you are having problems working with pupils – ask for advice. You may find that other TAs and teachers have had similar problems and can give helpful suggestions.

Active listening techniques can be helpful in supporting pupils who are having difficulties

To support pupils a TA needs to listen to what they are saying. We spend much of our working life talking and listening. But **active listening** is a special skill where we really focus on trying to understand what an individual pupil is saying. Active listening can be helpful in dealing with pupils who are having difficulties. Pupils who are having difficulties might seem unhappy, they may not be doing their work or they may seem reluctant to tell you why they are not doing their work. In working with such pupils you often need to read between the lines; this is where active listening becomes useful (see page 70).

Active listening involves sending positive body and voice messages

Positive body and voice messages tell the pupils that we are interested in what they have to say. Positive body language involves having a relaxed posture, leaning slightly forward, facing the pupil, maintaining a comfortable level of eye contact and using appropriate facial expressions. Sometimes it is useful to mirror facial expressions. If the pupil seems concerned, then we should be concerned. With very young children it is important to get down to their level. In terms of a pupil's personal space, getting too close physically may make the pupil feel uncomfortable or be perceived as threatening; however, if too far away, the pupil may see you as being emotionally distant. In terms of voice messages we need to pay attention to the volume of our voice. Too loud a voice and we may be seen as threatening; too soft a voice and we may be seen as weak.

Say important things in private

Obviously it is important that we are aware of others around us. Some discussions and statements are better said in private. Sometimes it is possible to go outside the classroom or to find a quiet place. If this is not possible and you feel that it is important to have a quiet chat in private, say to the pupil that you will talk about this later, but don't forget to have this chat.

Active listening involves respecting the speaker

Respecting the speaker involves trying to understand the world from the pupil's point of view. On a practical side this means putting aside your views and ideas and not interrupting the pupil but letting them have their say before you respond.

Active listening involves verbal techniques

Verbal techniques such as the use of openers, small rewards and open-ended questions are designed to encourage the pupil to open up. These techniques are very useful if the pupil is reluctant to talk.

Openers, as the name suggests, give the pupil permission to talk, e.g. 'You haven't started your worksheet, is everything all right?'

Small rewards are brief verbal and non-verbal responses you give to pupils to communicate to them that you are listening and that you are interested in what they have to say. These small rewards include nods, eye contact and soothing voice sounds such as 'mmm…'.

Once the pupil does begin to talk, open-ended questions, i.e. questions that require more than a yes or no response, encourage the pupil to keep talking. It is also important when encouraging pupils to talk that they do not feel rushed and that you do not bombard them with questions. Here the art is accepting silences and giving the pupils time to answer any questions you have asked them.

Active listening involves rewording and reflecting

Rewording involves listening to what the pupil has said and then rephrasing and repeating back to the pupil what they have just said. This is useful in that it helps you to understand what the pupil has just said and it communicates to the pupil that you are listening. Sometimes it is useful to *reflect feelings*, especially if there is a mismatch between the pupil's body language and what they are saying. A further advanced technique would be to reflect back to the pupil possible *reasons for their feelings*. These techniques are shown in the following example:

PUPIL: Can't understand. Can't.

TA: You can't understand the question. (*Here the TA is rewording or rephrasing what the pupil has said.*)

PUPIL: Yeah I don't care. (*Pupil has tears in their eyes.*)

TA: You say you don't care (*rephrasing*) but there are tears in your eyes so maybe you do care. (*Reflecting feelings.*) Maybe you are upset because you have tried really hard and it is still very difficult. (*TA reflecting a possible reason for the feelings.*) These questions are really difficult. Why don't we have a go together?

A positive relationship involves the pupil seeing the TA's help as *supportive*.

As a TA you will notice that while some pupils are very eager to accept your support, others will be very clear that they do not want your help and will say so in no uncertain terms. This can be a very difficult situation, especially if that uncooperative pupil is the one you are required to support. Though you may be there to help the pupil, they may see your help as proof that they cannot do the task and that they are somehow different from the other pupils. It is very important to be aware of how pupils see your support. This involves the active listening skills discussed earlier.

A gentle approach is needed with pupils who do not want to be supported

If a pupil clearly states that they do not want your help there are several strategies you can take. If the pupil definitely does need support you could offer support to those pupils nearby. You could involve the reluctant pupil in a group, which you support, and initially focus your attention on the other members. In this way the pupil is hearing the necessary extra information but not in a way that singles them out as different. Sometimes you will find that a pupil who usually accepts support all of a sudden refuses help. In some cases it is helpful to assure the pupil that you are there if needed and to give them space. A discussion with the pupil regarding their attitude will be necessary but such a discussion will need to be sensitively handled and conducted at a suitable time and place. Remember, important things are best said in private.

Questioning techniques

The skilful use of questions can enhance learning

The use of questions can serve many purposes:

- Questions can be used to check understanding.
- Questions can be used to revise and review previously taught material.
- Questions can be used as a means of gaining attention.

- Questions can be used to encourage thinking.
- Questions can be a way of drawing into the conversation the shyer members of the class. However, when asking a pupil who is shy, cautious or lacking in self-esteem, it is important to ask them a question that you are confident that they can answer. A question answered correctly and suitably praised will be a boost to their confidence and hopefully encourage that pupil to attempt to answer further questions.

Take time to think about the type of questions you ask pupil

How many questions do you ask? If you ask too many questions all at once pupils might become confused regarding which question they should be thinking about.

Do you give pupils enough time to think about the question or do you end up answering the question yourself? As a rule of thumb ask one question and give the pupil a few seconds to reply before you attempt to rephrase the question.

If pupils are not responding to your questions, are your questions phrased in language that the pupils can understand? Asking the question 'What calculations were we working on last session?' is probably fine for secondary pupils, but certainly not for pupils in the early years. Sometimes if the pupils are not answering the question it is helpful to break the question into smaller sub-questions eventually leading back to the initial question. For example, 'How did the story about the castle make you feel?' could be rephrased as 'What happened in the story? How do ghosts make you feel? How did the story about the castle make you feel?'

Do you always ask the same pupils? Do the same pupils always volunteer to answer? There is some evidence to suggest that teachers tend to pay attention more to boys than girls during classroom activities. It is important to try to encourage all pupils to participate.

Take time to think about how you respond to the answers pupils give to questions

What do you say to the pupil who gives an unexpected or incorrect response?

If this happens it is helpful to try to link the pupil's responses to some aspect of the lesson or another related question if possible. This will involve a certain amount of thinking on your feet but can have the advantage of boosting self-esteem and encouraging pupils to answer future questions.

For example:

TA: What is 7 add 5? Right Mary you have your hand up.
MARY: 2.
TA: Mary, that would be the correct answer if we were working out 7 take away 5, and we were doing subtraction yesterday. But what if we were adding the numbers?
MARY: 12.

Here the TA linked Mary's incorrect answer to a successful answer for a different question.

A further more advanced skill in questioning involves linking pupils' answers; this has the effect of showing the pupils that you value their contribution.

For example:

> John said that the book about the castle had a ghost in it. Rebecca said that on holiday she visited a castle that had 23 ghosts, but that she wouldn't want to stay there at night. However Leon said that the ghost in the book was a very friendly and helpful ghost. So how would we feel about visiting the castle in the book?

Self-esteem

TAs have a role in developing the self-esteem of the pupils with whom they work

Self-esteem is another word for self-evaluation. In our minds we have an image of how we are, *self-image*, and an image of how we would like to be, *ideal-self*. Self-esteem or self-evaluation involves comparing the way we are to the way we would like to be. In doing this evaluation we are likely to look at how intelligent we are, how many friends we have, any special skills we possess and what type of person we are. The combination of self-image, ideal-self and self-esteem forms our view of our self. One view of the development self has it that the self develops through everyday interactions. In these day-to-day interactions we become aware of how others see us and we make comparisons between others and ourselves. In fact by the age of 6 children will begin to make social comparisons and will be able to tell you who is the cleverest in the class. For example, 'Jody is better at maths than me as she is in the yellow group, but I am better than Lisa as she is in the green group.' (See pages 70, 72, 79).

The teaching profession today is more aware of the negative effects of labelling (e.g. 'He will never amount to anything') and the difficulties in streaming or placing pupils into ability groups (i.e. top, middle, bottom set). The teaching profession is aware of self-fulfilling prophecies whereby pupils live up or down to the expectations that others have of them.

TAs have a role to play in helping pupils feel good about themselves and helping all pupils believe that they can succeed as learners.

TAs also have a role to play in challenging negative stereotypes such as girls can't play football, boys can't cook or only boys are good at computers.

Pupils with high and low self-esteem will differ in a number of ways

It is the role of the TA to help all pupils to feel good about themselves; however, some pupils need more help with this than others. As such it is helpful to be able to identify those with high-self esteem and those with low self-esteem.

Pupils with high self-esteem:

- Are able to recognise their strengths and weaknesses.
- Are willing to work at what they find difficult.
- Can recognise other pupils' strengths and praise them for these.
- Are happy with who they are.
- Can work with pupils who are outside their friendship groups.
- Like challenges.
- Do not give up when things do not go as planned.
- Accept responsibility when they make mistakes.

Pupils with low self-esteem:

- Have difficulties in recognising their strengths and accepting their weaknesses.
- Are unwilling to work at things they find difficult.
- Would rather do nothing than do something and fail.
- Find it difficult to acknowledge others' strengths; are often jealous; will put down or criticise others in an attempt to make themselves feel good.
- Will often boast, show off, need to be the centre of attention. These behaviours may be an attempt to make themselves feel better.
- May rely on friends, teachers and others as they lack confidence in their own abilities.
- May have difficulties with relationships as they find it hard to trust.

- Find it difficult to take personal responsibility ('not my fault') and tend to blame others when they make mistakes or things go wrong.

This list shows that pupils who may appear confident, in that they boast or show off, may actually be lacking in self-esteem.

A TA can raise a pupil's self-esteem in day-to-day interactions

As a TA, you can:

- Communicate to the pupils the high expectations that you have for them. Let the pupils know that you believe in them.
- Think positively about the pupils you work with. Find something that you like in even those pupils who are most difficult to work with.
- Make a point of saying hello to pupils when you meet them around the school.
- Remind the pupils of what they are good at.
- Find out what the pupils' interests are. Talk to the pupils about their interests. Show the pupils that you like them.
- Praise the pupil regularly, but be sure that the praise is genuine.
- Find some aspect that the pupil has done well even if they have not succeeded at the task. Use the 4–1 rule: that is, for every one correction that you find tell them four things that they have succeeded at.
- Praise effort as well as achievement.
- Remind pupils of previous times when they have struggled and succeeded when they are experiencing difficulties.
- Let the pupils know that making mistakes is not only 'all right', but also part of the learning process.
- Tell the pupils of the mistakes that you have made and how you have learnt from them and how these mistakes have made you a better person.
- Use humour: 'It's good, but it's not right!'

Learning styles

A knowledge of pupil learning styles can be useful in supporting learning

Learning styles can be defined as different and preferred ways in which children and adults think and learn. Most pupils can learn when information is presented in a variety of formats and can learn in a variety of settings and circumstances. However, some pupils who have difficulty in learning, possibly many of those that you as a TA are supporting, can only learn in certain ways. A knowledge of the learning styles of the pupils you support can help you match your **teaching strategy** to the individual needs of the pupil. In identifying learning styles you could ask pupils how they learn best or you could get them to fill in various questionnaires (see Additional Resources). However, a knowledge of learning styles can also be obtained by observing over time how the pupil you support learns. To identify learning styles you will need to know the defining characteristics of each. This brings us to the next section. (See also pages 36–7, 45, 61, 77).

Identifying perceptual style – the visual, auditory and kinaesthetic learner

One of the most widely known learning styles refers to perceptual style, i.e. how pupils prefer to take in and process information through their senses. This view sees learners as **visual**, **auditory** or **kinaesthetic**.

Visual learners prefer learning through seeing and watching. For this type of learner, information is better remembered if presented in a visual format, e.g. pictures, maps and videos.

Auditory learners prefer learning through hearing and listening to information. This type of learner will retain information more readily if the information is heard. Information could be presented through lectures, tapes or within music.

Kinaesthetic learners need to be physically involved in the learning process. This type of learner prefers hands-on activities, such as projects, models or puzzles.

Much attention is given to this view of learning within schools and it is common for teachers to talk about how they 'VAK' their lesson plans; that is, how they adapt their lesson plans for visual, auditory and kinaesthetic learners.

Identifying physiological learning styles – preferences in time of day, food intake and degree of movement

Time of day refers to whether we are larks or owls: do we learn better in the morning or do we learn better at night? Food intake reflects the reality that some individuals feel that drinking or eating actually helps them to learn. Some individuals will state that they need to drink coffee or chew gum in order to concentrate. In terms of degree of movement, some individuals will say that in order to learn they need to sit still and focus. Others will say that moving around, fiddling with a pen, rocking backwards and forwards on a chair or doodling helps them to concentrate.

Of course the difficulty with implementing this learning style is that schools will have set routines of when certain subjects are taught, have expectations that pupils should remain in their seat and will have rules regarding eating and drinking in the classroom.

Identifying preferences in processing information

The global vs. analytic pupil

This learning style refers to how a pupil prefers to have new information presented to them. A global learner needs to see the big picture, i.e. to have an overview of the new topic before they can focus on the details. For an analytic learner the presentation of too much information too quickly is confusing and overwhelming. An analytic learner prefers information to be presented in an ordered and step-by-step fashion. They need to start at the beginning and work in a systematic way until they reach the conclusion.

The impulsive vs. reflective pupil

This learning style refers to how much time an individual chooses to think about a task before they actually begin it. A pupil with an impulsive learning style wants to jump right in (see page 96). The difficulty with this style is that in the desire to start and finish quickly the pupil might not have read the questions properly or have heard all of the instructions. This can often lead to unnecessary and careless mistakes. On the other hand, a pupil with a reflective learning style likes to sit back and think before they start. This pupil does not like to be rushed. However, though such a pupil will not be prone to careless mistakes, they might have difficulty in finishing the task in the set time.

Preference in background noise, temperature, classroom design and lighting

In terms of background noise, some pupils will say that they need absolute quiet while others will say that background noise or listening to music helps them to concentrate. In terms of temperature, some pupils prefer an airy, brisk, if not cold, classroom, while others need to feel warm to study effectively. In terms of classroom design, some pupils prefer to sit at a traditional desk and chair, while others like an informal environment in a circle or in groups. Still others prefer to sit on couches or the floor. In terms of lighting, some pupils prefer bright light while others prefer soft dim light.

Some pupils might complain that the sun is making it too bright for them to work while others love to sit and bask in the rays.

With regard to this learning style, it would be difficult to please all pupils at all times because, whatever the classroom environment, some will say: 'it's too quiet, it's too noisy, I can't work because I'm too hot, I can't work because I'm too cold'. However, this aspect needs careful consideration if the pupil has specific learning needs (see **autistic spectrum disorders (ASD)**, pages 85–7, visual impairments, page 106, and hearing impairments, pages 100–101).

Preferences in responsibility, degree of structure and who to work with

Degree of responsibility refers to the degree of adult supervision, feedback and guidance a pupil requires. This can be none, some or frequent.

Degree of structure refers to how the learning tasks are set out. Some pupils prefer tasks that are well structured; they need to be told exactly what to do and how to do it. If these pupils did not have a structure they wouldn't know where to begin. Some pupils prefer a less structured task, in that they are given an objective but they are also given choices in regard to how they should set about doing the task. These pupils could do a highly structured task but may find it stifles their creative nature.

Some pupils like to work by themselves, others like to be part of a team or a group and yet others like to work with an adult or authority figure. In addition some pupils like variety in who they work with and what they work on, while others like or need rigid routines (see ASD, pages 85–7, and **attention deficit hyperactivity disorder (ADHD)**, pages 81–4).

How to use individual learning styles to support pupils

VAK your sessions

As stated, it is now common for teachers to talk about how they 'VAK' their lesson plans, i.e. how they adapt their lesson plans for visual, auditory and kinaesthetic learners. As a TA you will often be working with small groups or on a one-to-one basis. If you know the preferred learning style of the pupils you support you can modify the task accordingly. For example, if the pupils you support in a maths session are having difficulties with the worksheet and you know that the pupils are visual or kinaesthetic learners, then the use of visual material, plastic money, counters, multi-link or numeracy games can be used. Teaching strategies using visual and hands-on material will match the learning styles of visual and kinaesthetic learners.

Keeping fidgety pupils in their seats

Of course the difficulty with working with pupils who as part of their learning style like to move around is that the teacher expects them to stay in their seats. Some TAs have found that if such a pupil is offered a piece of paper and a pen and allowed to doodle then they will actually sit and listen. However, it is always necessary to talk this through with the teacher beforehand. The last thing you want is for the teacher to tell the pupil off for doodling when you have just given them the paper and pen.

Finding a balance for the extremely impulsive or reflective pupil

A pupil who is very impulsive needs to slow down and think about the task. A TA can offer guidance in this by writing down the steps that a pupil needs to take before they begin the task. This could be done in the form of a checklist:

Step 1: Read the question.
Step 2: Think about what the question is asking. Do I understand what I should be doing?
Step 3: Start answering the question.
Step 4: Check my answer. Have I answered the question?

A pupil who is extremely reflective does need to work a little more quickly. As a TA you could encourage the pupil to limit how much time they spend thinking before they actually start the question.

Changing the environment to suit the pupil

With regard to environmental learning style, it would be difficult to please all pupils at all times. However, if you are working on a one-to-one basis, and if you are working outside the classroom, it might be possible to try and find that one special environment that suits the pupil. Sometimes, owing to lack of space, there are limited options. However, if you find that when working with your group in the library other pupils coming and going are producing too much of a distraction for your pupils then this does need to be discussed with the relevant teachers.

Though seating arrangements might be difficult to alter within a secondary classroom where many classes and teachers are sharing the same classroom, it might be useful to discuss seating plans with the teacher.

Teaching styles

Identify your own teaching style

Teaching styles can be described as your personal belief regarding how pupils learn. Your own teaching style is often a reflection of your own unique learning style and your experiences of being taught. So, if given a choice regarding how to teach, you would probably teach in a manner that reflects how you would like to be taught; that is, in a manner that matches your preferred learning styles.

One view of teaching styles describes the degree to which pupils are involved in the teaching process. Here a *formal approach* sees the teacher as the holder of all knowledge. This approach has the teacher talking about the subject usually at the front of the class with the pupils listening attentively. This approach has little pupil involvement. This style of teaching could suit an auditory learner.

The next approach is still *teacher centred* but the teacher aims to involve the pupils by providing demonstrations and modelling skills to be learned. This approach could suit a visual learner.

A more *pupil-centred approach* would see the teacher as a *facilitator* designing activities and group work to allow the pupil to become involved in the learning process. This approach, depending on the activities involved, could suit a kinaesthetic learner. An even more pupil-centred approach to teaching would involve the teacher giving the pupils the learning objectives (e.g. practise addition) and allowing the pupils to design their own learning tasks (e.g. design your own worksheet).

Another element of teaching styles is to describe the amount of control the teacher chooses to have over the class. A teacher who is *authoritarian* establishes strict rules and expects total obedience. A teacher who is *permissive* establishes few rules and is inconsistent in enforcing the rules that they do have. Finally a teacher who is *democratic* has rules but involves the pupils in deciding what the rules should be.

A further element of teaching styles relates to how information is communicated. This relates to the global vs. analytic learner. A *global teaching style* would have the teacher jumping from one concept to the next in order to provide the big picture. The *sequential teaching style* would prefer to present new information in an ordered step-by-step fashion.

Adapt the teaching style to the pupils you are teaching

The first point to remember is to be aware of what your teaching and learning styles are. Then as a TA you need to be aware of the learning styles of the pupils you support. It is important to be aware that your preferred teaching or learning styles would not necessarily match the learning styles of the pupils you are supporting.

At times you will need to adapt your teaching styles for different groups. At some times a teaching-centred approach involving demonstrations might be particularly suitable, e.g. when introducing new concepts in science. The amount of pupil involvement you would encourage within an activity would vary with the mix of pupils you are working with. For those pupils who need to know exactly what they should be doing, a very direct approach is needed. However, with pupils who want to express their creativity a pupil-centred approach, whereby you give them the freedom to design their learning tasks or make comments about how they would like to learn, is useful.

In terms of control, possibly there will be groups where, at least to begin with, you might need to adopt an authoritarian approach, where there are firm rules that need to be obeyed. However, in many groups, allowing pupils to establish their own group rules (taking a democratic approach) is very effective.

It is easy to adapt your learning or teaching styles if you are working with one pupil, but what do you do if you are working with pupils who have a variety of learning styles? All you can do in this case is to vary your approach, hopefully catering for all of the pupils at least some of the time.

How to manage your time in order to support pupils

TAs need to prioritise

The difficulty of how to manage your time effectively arises when you are working with a group of mixed ability pupils or working in a secondary school supporting several pupils who are seated in various corners of the room. The question that arises frequently in these situations is, 'Who do I support first?' Your first task as a TA is to get pupils started on the activity. Start with the pupil who needs the most support. Tell the pupils that they will all have their turn but that they need to be patient. Sometimes having pupils work in pairs is helpful. Though, saying that, attention needs to be given to which pupils would work most effectively together.

How to motivate pupils

Give praise

Praise in order to be effective must be genuine and must be seen as genuine by the pupil. Praise needs to be specific. For example, 'Well done! You did

very well in remembering to put full stops at the end of all your sentences.'
It is also important to praise effort as well as achievement.

Set tasks that are achievable

Remember, it is much easier to give praise if the set tasks are within the
capabilities of the pupil. Check to ensure that the pupils understand what
they should be doing. Check to see if they have the necessary skills to
complete the assignment. If they do not, talk to the teacher regarding more
appropriate work.

Make work relevant

There are certainly times in secondary school where pupils will ask, 'Why
do I have to know this information?' At such times it is helpful to relate
information to be learnt to practical everyday life. Sometimes information
that you have regarding the pupils' personal interests can help. If a pupil
complains that maths is boring and useless but you know that they would
like to be a builder when they get older, you can talk about how basic
maths is necessary in calculating costs or measuring the dimensions of
rooms.

Give the pupils strategies for increasing their motivation

If the pupils say the work is boring, or fall asleep while trying to read the
text, give them strategies for increasing their motivation. Ask them if they
can find a way of relating what they are reading to their own interests.
Suggest that, as they read, rather than read passively they ask themselves
questions about the text.

How to encourage independent learning

Teachers often report that it is very important for them to know how much
of the pupils' work is their own and how much work is the TA's. Therefore
in feedback to the teacher it is very important to specify what the pupil has
accomplished and how much help, assistance and prompting was given.
Though a TA is there to support pupils, the ultimate aim is to give them
the skills and confidence to become independent learners. This can be
accomplished in everyday interactions. For example, when a pupil asks how
to spell a word, the easiest thing to do would be to give them the answer,
but it would be more beneficial to instruct them in finding ways to solve
the problem themselves. A pupil who does not know how to spell a certain

word could look in a dictionary. As a TA you could remind pupils of where the dictionaries are located and how to use them. Even with those pupils who need much support, you will need to move gradually to a point where they take on more of the work for themselves.

Supporting pupils to complete homework assignments

Help the pupil to use a homework diary

Homework becomes more important as the pupil progresses through the school system. Ensure that the pupil you are supporting has written down the appropriate homework. To begin with you might need to write this down.

Ask the pupil about where they do their homework

Sometimes pupils have difficulties with homework due to the fact that they have nowhere appropriate to study. Ask them about where they do their homework. If home is not the ideal place then suggest to them that they might want to attend a homework club.

Talk about time-management skills

If the pupil has exams or coursework to do, encourage the pupil to set aside the necessary time to revise. Revising at the last minute, or doing coursework the night before it is due in, is rarely successful. Have the pupil work backwards from the time that the work is due in and set aside blocks of time. In working out a schedule for work it is very important that the schedule is realistic. Working three hours straight on biology might be possible but it is more likely that the pupil will find it easier to work in one-hour slots.

Encourage the pupil to reward themselves

Suggest to the pupil that they give themselves rewards for working hard, e.g. perhaps half an hour on a favourite video game.

Break a complicated task into small steps

A 500-word essay on 'Discuss and evaluate research on global warming', for example, might seem very daunting, but if broken down into introduction, discussing the research, evaluating the research and stating the conclusions, then the task begins to become more manageable.

Help the pupil to work out priorities

If the pupil feels overwhelmed with the amount they have to do, help them decide on what work is the most important to do.

Checklist

✓   Use active listening skills when communicating with pupils.
✓   Be familiar with different types of questioning techniques.
✓   Do everything you can to raise a pupil's self-esteem.
✓   Modify work to take into account individual learning styles.
✓   Give pupils the skills to manage time, complete homework and to become independent learners.

4   Strategies for supporting literacy

This chapter relates mainly to supporting literacy in the primary school. However, many of the principles can be applied to other lessons in primary schools and to secondary schools.

The National Literacy Strategy

What is the National Literacy Strategy?

Over recent years the government has developed the **National Literacy Strategy (NLS)** in order to promote the learning and teaching of literacy in primary schools throughout the country. The fundamental platform in this strategy is the '**Literacy Hour**'. Each Literacy Hour should give time for preparation, study and reflection. There is to be space for whole-class teaching, pupils working independently and collaborative group work. The expectation is that the majority of pupils will be able to access the curriculum and keep up with the pace so that they progress and leave their primary phase of education with basic literacy skills well established.

Differentiation and additional support

Not all pupils, however, will be able to leave primary school with established literacy skills. Recognising this, the government speaks of additional support being provided at a level appropriate to children's needs. This support is described in terms of 'Waves'.

Wave One is support within the classroom through **differentiation**. Essentially, differentiation means adapting the work for the individual pupil, simplifying it for those who would otherwise find the work difficult and giving extension activities for more able pupils. Wave Two is 'catch-up' programmes to be delivered to small groups of pupils who are one or two terms behind the expected norm and who should, with this support, make up the ground. Wave Three support is more intensive programmes which may be delivered to small groups or to individual pupils, depending on their level of need.

'Wave One' TA support within the literacy hour

As a TA, you can support pupils within the literacy hour during every phase of the lesson.

The TA's role within whole-class activities

When whole-class learning is taking place, you can position yourself near to pupils who may find listening and participating in class discussion difficult. When working with younger children this may involve actually sitting on the floor with them, depending on how the teacher organises the lesson. Whether on the floor or sitting on a chair, you are in a position to help individual pupils focus on what is taking place.

A whole range of activities are available to you. These are some examples, but there are, of course, many more and they apply in many more lessons than the Literacy Hour:

- You can help pupils understand what is being said by repeating it in simplified language.
- You can help the pupil formulate their own answers to questions.
- You can quietly remind them of what they have learnt previously, ensuring the rest of the class is not disturbed.
- You can use visual stimuli with children, although this is often hard to do in practice.
- You can keep a pupil who is easily distracted focused on the lesson.
- If you are working with a child with a hearing or visual impairment, you can use signing or adapted resources to help them connect with what is happening (see pages 100–101, 106).

Many primary teachers and an increasing number of secondary teachers give each pupil an A4-sized personal whiteboard on which they can write any comments, thoughts or answers. If the teacher you are working with has organised the class in this way, you can support by helping children spell words on their whiteboards, by scribing for those who find writing hard or laborious, or suggesting ideas which the pupils may like to consider.

Participating in structured or informal observations

It may be that you have been asked by the teacher to monitor particular pupils during whole-class teaching. This is a vital role and one which the teacher, with responsibility for the entire class, may find difficult to do. You can observe the pupils and note down their responses to the lesson; for instance, how many times they participate in discussions, what sort of answers and contributions they make, how often they are distracted and so on. A picture gained in this way will show to what extent they understand what is happening and how much they are gaining from the lesson. Based on your observations, an intervention programme might be drawn up to support a pupil in a more focused way. Part of your observation may also be noting how particular pupils are meeting specific targets set in their IEPs. This is an invaluable part of assessing a pupil's progress (see pages 2, 18–19, 69).

A TA's role in group and independent work

Your role in this part of the lesson, as in all lessons, is to help pupils relate to what is being taught and enable them to learn as much as they can. Depending on how the class is organised, you may find yourself sitting at a table with a group of children who find it difficult to work at the same pace or to the same level as most of the rest. Alternatively, you may be asked to support those who are progressing at a faster rate than most. Or you may be working with pupils who are coping well with the content and pace of the lesson and your job is to help them consolidate and generalise what they know. It may be that you will not be allocated to one particular group at all, but will be expected to move around the class, supporting pupils as and when they need it. Over the course of a few weeks, ideally, you should find yourself being asked to provide support in each and every one of these ways. Within a secondary school, you might be supporting several pupils who have IEPs but who are seated at various places in the class (see pages 2, 18–19, 69).

Whatever the case, it is essential that this support is planned with the teacher before the lesson. It is all too easy to assume that, because you are in the room, you will know what to do and what you do will be what the teacher wants you to do, and that what you do will be of most benefit to the pupils. However, planning time is not always easy to achieve, particularly in secondary schools. Nevertheless, it is important to try and have a discussion with the teacher before the lesson commences. TAs often say that if they know in advance what the class will be learning, they feel in a stronger position to support pupils (see page 7).

When working with a group of whatever ability you can:

- Ensure that all pupils understand what is being asked of them and can read any materials that have been handed out.
- Go over the teaching points made earlier in the lesson, taking time to give more explanation if that is needed.
- Facilitate pupils working with each other by 'chairing' discussions.
- Guide pupils in their own reading and writing.
- Keep pupils focused on the task in hand.
- Provide adapted resources when needed, such as sloping boards, larger print materials, triangular pens and pencils, simplified dictionaries, spellcheckers.
- Work with pupils using word processors.
- Help pupils express their ideas through *mind-maps* (Buzan and Buzan, 1993; Buzan, 2003).
- Prepare pupils to participate in the plenary, which offers the opportunity for feedback and reflection and preparation for the next lesson.

'Wave Two' TA support – catch-up programmes

Wave Two intervention programmes include the government's 'Early Literacy Support' (ELS) for Key Stage One, 'Additional Literacy Support' (ALS) for Key Stage Two, particularly Years 3 and 4, and 'Further Literacy Support' (FLS) for Key Stage Two, particularly Years 5 and 6. These programmes often emphasise the teaching of **phonics**. Schools are not required to use these programmes, but they are required to meet the needs of all pupils. If schools choose not to use these actual programmes, they must be able to show that what they are using is as effective in helping children 'catch up'.

Although, technically, such programmes are not 'special needs provision', they are usually delivered by TAs. This will require you to work outside of the classroom with a small group of pupils. To deliver these programmes, and others like them, you will need to receive training, in both the content of the programmes and how they are to be taught, monitored and progress recorded. You should never be 'thrown in at the deep end' and be given half-a-dozen pupils and told to get on with it.

'Wave Three' TA support – intervention programmes

For those pupils who are a year or more behind the expected level, more intensive levels of support will usually need to be provided, and, again, the TA plays a crucial role in the delivery of this support.

Such support comes under the definition of 'special educational provision' and may be given to small groups or to individual pupils, as the need expresses itself. Often, but not always, this support is delivered both within and outside of the class. The issue of withdrawing pupils from the class is controversial. Some argue that such withdrawal does no good whatsoever as it removes the pupil from the situation where the problem arises. The pupil may make progress in the individual tuition situation, but not be able to apply this knowledge within the classroom. Proponents of withdrawal see things differently and stress the value of being able to teach small groups or individuals in a more intensive and 'tailored' way. Whatever the theoretical arguments, you may well be asked to work in just such a situation.

In the primary sector, there are many published small-group or individual intervention programmes designed to teach the basics of literacy and which are to be delivered outside of the classroom. Most teach reading, spelling, **phonology**, phonics, and so on in small, structured steps with a great deal of reinforcement and use a variety of methods to relate best to the learning styles of pupils (see pages 31–5). Many programmes state that they are **multi-sensory**. This means that they seek to employ at least the senses of sight, touch and hearing in the learning process (see page 56). Intervention programmes are usually more effective if delivered in short but frequent sessions.

What TAs need to know

If you are required to support pupils with such programmes, there are a number of things to be borne in mind:

- Before you begin, ensure you are thoroughly familiar with the scheme.
- You need to know what its aims are – where it is heading.
- You need to know how it is designed to be delivered.
- You will need to know exactly when and where you will be able to deliver this programme.
- You will need to know how the intervention is to be monitored and by whom.
- You need to know what records you are to keep.
- You need to know where you are to store any resources, equipment and work produced by the pupils.
- You will need to know your responsibilities in dealing with any inappropriate behaviour within the group you are going to work with.

- You should know what is happening for these pupils in the class as well so that you can tailor the programme as much as possible to fit in with that.
- You need to know what your responsibilities are regarding the parents of the pupils in your group.
- You need to know what to do if you feel a particular programme is proving to be inappropriate for a pupil.

All this should be discussed and agreed upon by teachers, the SENCO and yourself before you start working with individual pupils on intensive support programmes.

Supporting pupils who have English as an additional language (EAL)

Distinguish between EAL and SEN

You may be asked to support pupils for whom English is not their first language. For these pupils, where there is a difficulty with understanding and making progress in literacy the issue is likely to be one of language rather than an actual learning difficulty. It is vitally important to recognise the difference between issues of EAL and SEN.

When asked to support pupils who are new to English or who are struggling with the language, you need to know several things to help plan your support:

- What is the pupil's home language and how fluent are they in this?
- Are they literate in their home language, or do they only speak it?
- How long have they been in this country?
- How long have they been learning English?
- What education have they received prior to coming to this country or to your school?

If the pupils are refugees or asylum seekers there may be additional factors such as trauma and family break-up or loss which affect the learning process (see pages 74, 103).

You should never be expected to support such pupils without support for yourself either from within the school itself or from the LEA's services for ethnic minorities. Ideally, pupils newly arrived at school should be assessed by people who speak their first language. This will give the clearest indication possible of their level of fluency and literacy in their mother tongue.

The role of the TA

Strategies employed to support these pupils should normally be delivered within the class. It is strongly recommended that pupils new to English are placed with groups of fluent and able English speakers who can provide good role models. Your role as TA may be to explain particular vocabulary during the lesson, often using a bilingual dictionary. You may also be asked to teach basic vocabulary, in which case this is likely to happen outside of the class. Not least, your role is to be a listening and caring adult in the midst of a possibly strange and unintelligible environment.

The use of writing frames to assist pupils in writing

What are 'writing frames'?

When confronted with an entirely blank sheet of paper and asked to write on it, many pupils, and adults too for that matter, go blank themselves. Whatever was in their head goes completely out of it and they do not know where to begin. Using writing frames can help overcome this initial reluctance to write by providing a simple structure around which pupils can develop their ideas. A writing frame can be as simple as a border around the page, but more often it is more complex. Examples are given in Tables 3.1, 3.2 and 3.3(a) and (b), in the Appendix.

As with all resources, some forethought needs to be given to the writing frames and they need to be prepared beforehand. Pupils will need to be taught how to use them effectively. The idea is that, by using writing frames initially, pupils who are reluctant to write will learn how to frame their writing for themselves.

Writing frames can be used in the classroom as part of the differentiated resources at the disposal of the teacher or the TA. They do not highlight the learning needs of individuals and can actually be introduced to the whole class so that all pupils get to use them.

Because they are so easy to make, there is an infinite variety of writing frames which can be created and adapted for specific tasks by teachers and TAs. Older children can be encouraged to create their own using their developing IT skills.

Tips for improving reading

To support children in their reading it is not sufficient simply to listen to them read. On the other hand, unless you do listen to them read it is difficult to know how much progress they are making. Within the busy school day it is often very hard to find time to listen to readers, but such time must be made. Like everything else, it must be planned for. As a TA you may well be asked to listen to children of all abilities read, and you need to know how to make the most of this opportunity. There are a few 'rules' of which you need to be aware, particularly when working with reluctant readers.

Be positive

Never say to a pupil 'No, that was wrong' when they misread a word. They are probably doing their best and need no further discouragement when it comes to reading. Always be positive and ask questions like 'Does that word make sense?' or 'Do you think that sounds right?' or 'Can you think of a word this is more likely to be?' The idea is to help them come up with the correct response themselves by giving them strategies which they can use independently.

Variety is the key

The way children learn to read is complex, involving a combination of memorising whole words (learning sight vocabulary) and learning how words are made up (phonics). When helping any pupil struggling with reading, use a combination of these approaches to support them. At times, therefore, it is helpful to say 'Try and sound that word out' or 'What sound does the word begin with?', but this will not always be suitable. The trick is to vary your approach so the child picks up on a variety of strategies.

Pause–Prompt–Praise

If a child appears to be getting stuck on a word, remember *Pause–Prompt–Praise*. When they hesitate, you pause – do not be too quick to jump in with a correction or comment. Some say you need to give pupils 10 seconds to try and work a word out. If, after this time, they remain unable to read the word, or if they make a mistake and do not realise it, give a prompt by speaking out the first sound or the first syllable. This prompt may jog their memory and they give you the word. If they do not, give them the word and have them repeat it. Always praise them for their efforts and their response.

Develop a sight vocabulary

When working with younger children who are just developing their reading skills, this is perhaps all that you will need. Your aim is to promote fluency in reading rather than use every reading session as an opportunity to teach phonics. Initially you will be wanting to build up a basic **sight vocabulary** of common words. The National Literacy Strategy gives 45 'Reception Words' which are the most common words in the English written language, and 'Year 1–2 Words' are the next 115 most common words. It is useful for you to be aware of these words, but it is not necessarily helpful to try and teach them by rote out of the context of genuine reading.

Choose the right text

With children from Year 2 upwards, you may well need to begin by finding out whether the book they are reading is suitable for them. As a rule of thumb, if they read with 100 per cent accuracy, the book is too simple. If they make errors on more than 5 per cent of the text it is too difficult and they will probably not understand it. To develop fluency whilst at the same time helping children make progress in reading, they need to be reading around 98 per cent of words accurately. Your first means of support, therefore, is in helping them choose the books which are most suitable for them.

Assessing reading using a 'miscue analysis'

Once a suitable level of text has been established it can be helpful to undertake something called a **miscue analysis** (see page 97). This will help you identify patterns of errors or 'miscues' on the 2 per cent of words pupils find difficult to read. To do this you need to photocopy around 100 words of text, enlarging it so that you can make notes on it. Ask pupils to read that part of the text to you; note down on your photocopy any miscues they make. It may be that they hesitate, omit words or lines, repeat words, mispronounce words, misread the phonetic clues or whatever. You need to note above the word any mistake they make. At this stage, do not correct them; you are simply carrying out an initial assessment. Examples of common coding used in miscue analysis are as follows:

	'*bricks*'
Substitution	write the substitution above the text, e.g. 'bicycle'
No response	underline, e.g. <u>thatcher</u>
Insertion	put in oblique stroke (/) and write what was inserted

Omission   ring the word left out

Reversal   underline and write 'R' over the word reversed,
                            e.g. 'saw' read as 'was'

**Repetition of
word or phrase**   underline with dashes

Hesitation   put oblique stroke either side of word hesitated
                            over, e.g. /awkward/

**Phonic
attempts**   put a dash between each letter, e.g. s–p–l–a–sh

Self-correction   place a tick beside any previous comment

Once you have noted miscues on your copy of the text, you can begin to analyse patterns of errors. It may be that the pupil always misreads 'ch' for 'sh' or refuses to read words of more than two syllables. Where patterns emerge, make that the focus of your teaching and support. The point of miscue analysis is to know the ways pupils are misreading text and then to do something about it.

Developing phonological awareness

Fundamental to being able to read is the ability to distinguish sounds within words. This is phonology, and is the other side of the coin to phonics. Phonics is looking at symbols on paper (the letters of the alphabet) and being able to 'decode' their sounds. Phonology involves such things as being able to hear and create rhyme, alliteration, and distinguish syllables and phonemes within words.

A simple glossary of terms might be helpful at this point, for if you as a TA know what you are talking about, the chances are you will be able to help the pupils more effectively.

Phonemes

- The smallest units of sound that can affect meaning within a word.
- The 26 letters of the alphabet make 44 phonemes.

cat	ship	thought

- Each of the above words has three phonemes, even though they have three, four and seven letters respectively:

c–a–t	sh–i–p	th–ough–t

Onset

- The initial consonant or consonant cluster in a word. Words beginning with vowels do not have an onset.

Rime

- That part of a word which contains the vowel and final consonant cluster if there is one. Words beginning with vowels consist only of rime.

c–*at*	sh–*ip*	th–*ought*

Grapheme

- Written representation of a phoneme – what we normally call *letters*.

Syllables

In helping children distinguish **syllables** two tactile procedures can help. Each syllable is one beat in a word, so they can tap out the 'rhythm' of the word. Also, have them place their hands lightly under their chin. Each time they say a syllable their chin moves down. By using either of these two ways, children can count how many syllables there are in any word.

Technically a syllable is a part of a word which contains one and only one vowel sound. There may be more than one vowel, but there is only one vowel sound. This can help older children with their spellings, but does not need to be taught to younger children. Simply using beats in a word or the chin movement can be enough.

Terminology within phonics

It is also helpful to be aware of the correct terminology for phonics. This is certainly the case if you are going to deliver ELS, ALS or FLS:

- *Vowels* – the letters *a/e/i/o/u* and, when standing in for an /*i*/, the letter /*y*/. Every word and syllable contains a vowel sound. Each vowel has two sounds – a *long vowel sound*, such as the *a* in *mate*, and a *short vowel sound*, such as the *a* in *mat*.

- *Consonants* – all the other letters of the alphabet.
- *Blends* – two or more letters which run smoothly into each other whilst keeping their distinctive sounds, e.g. *st/spr/bl.*
- *Initial consonant blends* – two or more consonants forming blends at the beginning of words, e.g. *stop/spring/bleach.*
- *Final consonant blends* – two consonants forming blends at the end of words, e.g. lo*ft*/lo*st*/sp*ring.*
- *Digraphs* – two or more letters forming one sound which can be one of the following:

  - *Consonant digraphs* – two consonants forming one sound, *ch/sh/ th/wh.*
  - *Vowel digraphs* – two or more vowels forming one sound, e.g. *ee/ea/ou/ai.*
  - *Vowel–consonant digraphs* – two or more vowels and consonants forming one sound, e.g. *ar/er.*

Supporting pupils is all about motivating them to learn, and they are much more likely to be motivated by the concept of 'magic e' (e.g. the word *rat* with an 'e' on the end becomes *rate*) than having to learn about 'split vowel digraphs' – which is the same thing. So, do not get too hung-up on being technical.

Developing phonic skills

After your miscue analysis it may be that you have discovered the pupil does not understand or is not aware of some particular phonic skill. As part of your support to improve reading, you could specifically teach this skill and then help the pupil apply it in their reading. There are multitudes of published resources available to help you with this, but be careful: do not slavishly follow any publication; use only what you need; and, above all, avoid 'death by worksheets'.

Using coloured paper or overlays

Some children, particularly those with **dyslexia** (see pages 96–8), benefit from having text printed on coloured paper or from using coloured plastic overlays. Black print on white background often seems to 'move across the page' for these pupils, and coloured backgrounds or filters help prevent this. You need to experiment with different colours to find out which ones work best for the pupils you support.

Presentation of worksheets

When designing worksheets for your pupils, take care with the font and spacing. It is best to use fonts like Comic Sans or Infant Sassoon, which are clearer than Times New Roman or Arial. Leave sufficient space on the worksheet for pupils to read the instructions or information in an uncluttered way. Put enough on the sheet to stretch the pupils but not so much that they are unable to complete the task.

Tips for improving writing

Write for a purpose

When was the last time you wrote something simply because you were told to do so? As adults, we (mostly) get to choose when we write, what we write and why we write. For pupils in school this is not the case. Most of what children write is set for them by somebody else; and we wonder why many children find writing hard.

One of the essential factors in developing writing is to explain the reason for it. Part of your support will be to ensure children are writing for a purpose. As a TA you can be especially helpful in talking with individual pupils or with small groups, reinforcing the reason for writing, which should already have been introduced by the teacher.

If pupils are clear about why they are being asked to write something, motivation is likely to increase. If they feel they are being asked to write merely as a meaningless exercise, they are less likely to produce the goods.

Structuring and sequencing

You can talk with pupils and small groups, encouraging them to share their ideas verbally before committing them to paper. Your aim is to help pupils put their ideas into sequences which make sense, so that, for instance, when writing fictional stories, they construct their writing with a beginning, a middle and an end.

Story mountains

Many schools use a 'story mountain' to help pupils develop their creative writing. This is a line drawn in the shape of a mountain outline, with the sequence of events in the story beginning at the foot of the mountain on one side, climbing the mountain up that side, reaching the summit and then descending to the foot on the other side. The stages of this climb relate to:

- the beginning of the story, setting the scene at the start of the climb;
- developing the story, which often involves introducing a problem or an element of tension, on the way up one side of the mountain;
- reaching the summit with a climax which requires some kind of resolve;
- the resolution is on the way down the other side of the mountain, and may be interrupted by a second problem or element of tension requiring further resolution;
- finally ending with a conclusion which brings the story nicely down to the foot of the mountain on the other side.

Once pupils become familiar with structuring a story in this way, and can begin to identify how professional writers use similar structures in their writing, this can be a very helpful way of improving sequencing and shape in their own writing.

Collaborative work

Pupils working collaboratively, when they share ideas and offer peer support, can be very effective in improving writing. This is particularly the case for pupils with English as an additional language or for those experiencing barriers to learning when it comes to writing. Slow writers can be encouraged to share ideas verbally, whilst others note these down. As a TA working with a group you can facilitate such collaborative work, ensuring that each pupil has an opportunity to contribute and that no one or two children dominate the group.

One way you as a TA can facilitate such collaboration is to act as the scribe for the group as they discuss ideas or jointly edit their previous writing. Using a flipchart you can jot down their ideas and comments as they make them, thus giving them space to talk and share ideas and thoughts.

Stimulating writing

It is very difficult writing in a vacuum, so the teacher, for example, will almost certainly introduce some sort of stimuli to develop pupils' creative writing. As a TA you can reinforce such stimuli with individuals or small groups by asking how they felt when they heard, saw or touched the stimuli. You can help them by giving them vocabulary to describe these sensations.

Modelling the process of writing

Letting the children know how you yourself write, working it out with them, talking out loud as you do, can be a very effective way of improving writing. Children need to know how adults write, that there is a process involved and that it does not magically appear from nowhere.

Assessing writing

You may be asked to mark pupils' writing. If you are, do not cover the page with red ink. Remember that you are seeking to assess *for* learning, to help children learn, and not to point out all their mistakes. You therefore need to mark to the specific **learning objectives** of the lesson and you need to give pupils time for reflection on the marking and comments made. If, for instance, the object of the writing was to use adverbs effectively, highlight where these have been used and point out where they could have been used. It is not helpful to point out every single spelling or punctuation error.

Children need to focus on one thing at a time. There will be other opportunities to identify areas for improvement in spelling, punctuation or grammar.

How to help pupils overcome spelling difficulties

Why spelling can be difficult

It is not hard to understand why many pupils experience difficulty with spelling English words. Did you know, for instance, that the word GHOTI spells 'fish'? If you take the 'gh' in *enough*, the 'o' in *women*, and the 'ti' in *station* and put these together, you have *fish*. Simple, isn't it? In fact, despite the vagaries of English spelling, over 80 per cent of words follow definite spelling rules. The trouble is, there are so many rules.

Spelling rules and patterns

One of the ways you can help older pupils overcome spelling difficulties is to teach them some of the more common spelling rules. To do this, you need to be aware of the rules yourself. Most of us were probably taught *'i' before 'e' except after 'c'* at school, and some of us may have understood it, but we were unlikely to have been taught many other spelling rules. Did you know, for instance, that very few English words end in 'i' or that a 'w' always modifies the short vowel 'a' after it to sound like an 'o' but that it leaves the long vowel 'a' as an 'a'?

Another way to help older pupils is to show them the structure of words. In English, words are built around a 'base word' or 'root'. Prefixes and/or suffixes are added to the beginnings or ends of bases or roots to alter their meaning. Once pupils have learnt the base or root of the word and have become familiar with prefixes and suffixes, they can be encouraged to build up complex words for themselves.

A third way to help older pupils learn spellings is to teach them about short vowels and long vowels, open and closed syllables, and short-vowel and long-vowel patterns. It sounds more complex than it is, but it is not straightforward and there are always plenty of exceptions.

There are a number of resources available to you to help you in all this. One of the most useful is *Alpha to Omega* (Hornsby and Shear, 1993). Another is *Teaching Reading Through Spelling* (Cowdery *et al.*, 1983–5). The government's own documentation in the NLS is also very useful when it comes to spelling rules and patterns.

Strategies for difficult words

Help pupils learn patterns of words. This is far more successful than learning lists of random words by rote. If, for instance, a pupil is uncertain how to spell 'rain', it may be helpful to ask them to learn four or five words with the same vowel pattern, such as 'gain', 'main' and 'plain', alongside the target word 'rain'.

Help pupils see words within words such as 'ant' in 'elephant'.

Help pupils learn words by using a mnemonic, for instance: 'Big Elephants Can't Always Use Small Exits' for 'because'. Children enjoy making up their own. This can be particularly effective for tricky words like 'said' (see page 97).

Help pupils use a range of senses when learning their spellings (see page 45). Use wooden or plastic letters to set the words out. Use sand trays for pupils to write words with their fingers, or have pupils scribe words in large letters in the air. Use different colours to highlight words. Have pupils say the letters out loud as they write and copy them because we all remember what we hear ourselves say better than we remember what somebody else says to us. Have pupils write out the words with their eyes closed, saying the letters out loud. This can be an effective way of breaking inaccurate spelling habits as pupils have become accustomed to seeing themselves write in a certain way.

Always remember – give children space to make mistakes and to experiment with spellings for themselves. Your aim is to give them strategies so they can recognise spelling errors for themselves and correct them without your assistance.

Tips for improving handwriting

'Cheat'

Use a word processor, that's what most adults do.

Unfortunately, this simplistic response, attractive as it is, is inadequate when it comes to pupils in school, for they need to be able to express themselves legibly in writing.

Reasons for difficulties

How to help children improve their handwriting will to a large extent be dependent upon why they find handwriting difficult in the first place. Maybe they have so many ideas in their heads they want to get them down on paper quickly and they rush at it. If that is the case, simply getting them to slow down and to focus on handwriting will often be sufficient.

Be aware of dyspraxia

Some pupils have **dyspraxia,** now more technically described as **developmental coordination disorder** (see pages 89–91). If this is the case, there may be a physiological reason why their handwriting is so poor. Where this is the case, asking them to fill in countless worksheets copying handwriting patterns is worse than useless. In most cases this simply reinforces what they cannot do.

Use hand-gym

One effective way to help children improve their handwriting is to have them conduct what have become known as **hand-gym** exercises (see page 89). The aim is to develop muscle tone in their fingers, hands, wrists and arms, and, along the way, improve hand–eye coordination. Hand-gym is a series of daily physical exercises for the hands and fingers such as squeezing different-sized pegs between the fingers of both hands or rolling up strips of bandage with the fingers whilst the ball of the hand lies flat on the table.

Use games

Using printed mazes can be effective and fun. Ask children to trace a route in or out of mazes of varying complexity with a pencil without taking it off the paper or going through lines.

Having children make gross motor movements, making large patterns or letters in the air or on whiteboards, can also be effective. One of the reasons why children find it difficult to form letters accurately is that their larger muscles are not used to the movements required. By having them build these up, fine motor skills can be more easily improved.

How to help individuals who are left-handed

Difficulties experienced by left-handed writers

Pupils (and adults) who are left-handed experience different handwriting needs to those who are right-handed. Clearly, left-handed writers should not be made to stand out from the rest, but they may well need specific help with handwriting. As the child who is left-handed writes, their arm moves towards the body rather than away from it, which can be tiring. They may cover the words they have just written with their hand or arm which could result in smudging or forgetting what has been written. Their flow of writing is therefore likely to be interrupted as they stop to look over what they have just put onto paper.

What helps

The position of the paper is very important for a left-handed writer. It is usually most helpful to have the piece of paper or exercise book positioned to the left of the writer with it angled at about 45 degrees to the side of the desk. This will enable the writer to see the words as they are written and will minimise the likelihood of smudging.

Next, help the left-handed pupil to sit in a way which is the most relaxing for writing. Light should come from the right-hand side, otherwise the pupil will be working in their own shadow. If the pupil can be given a slightly higher chair this may also help as they will be able to look down more easily on their work. They need to sit to the right of the desk to give them space on their left and they need to sit to the left of other pupils so that their elbows do not clash.

Finally, the type of pen used is important. Left-handed writers benefit from using ball-point pens or roller-ball pens rather than fountain pens. A fountain pen tends to dig into the paper and blotch more readily for left-handed writers than for those who are right-handed. All pupils, but especially those who are left-handed, need to be taught to grip the pen or pencil relatively lightly and a couple of centimetres or so up from the point or nib. The most common grip is the 'tripod grip', where the pen or pencil is held in balance between the thumb and the first two fingers, but the left-handed writer must be allowed to find a grip which suits them (see page 91).

Some words of caution

Promote independence

Do not do the work for the pupil. Much like scaffolding on the outside of a tall house provides support for decorators, you are there to provide 'educational scaffolding' within which pupils can work for themselves. There is always a danger of over-reliance on a TA. Your role is to promote interaction between pupils. You should therefore seek to avoid the danger of pupils relating primarily, or even exclusively, to you in a lesson. This can be especially an issue if you are employed to work with an individual pupil who has a high level of dependence upon adult support.

Checklist

✓ 'Wave One' intervention provides support within the class.
✓ 'Wave Two' support may involve working with small groups of children outside of the class.
✓ 'Wave Three' intervention is likely to involve more intensive individual or small-group work.
✓ Numerous strategies and techniques to help improve reading and writing exist.
✓ The English language presents great difficulties to many pupils learning to spell; TAs can help overcome these difficulties.

5 Strategies for supporting numeracy

National Numeracy Strategy

What is the National Numeracy Strategy?

The **National Numeracy Strategy (NNS)** has been introduced to primary schools to boost levels within maths. One hour each day is to be given over to teaching maths in a structured way – whole-class teaching, followed by individual or group work and finishing with a whole-class plenary. The initial session can be used to review and reinforce work from previous lessons or to introduce new concepts. The plenary is an opportunity for reflection and consolidation.

The NNS identifies a number of mathematical objectives which should be achieved by the majority of pupils in any particular year group. It encourages teachers to use a variety of language and teaching methods so that pupils have the experience of more than one method of calculation. Teachers are required to allow pupils to record answers in differing ways, as suits them best.

Catch-up programmes

The government recognises that not all pupils will maintain the pace of the NNS, and has introduced a 'catch-up' programme for those needing to revisit work. This programme, called *Springboard*, sets out what is to be taught and how it is to be taught for each of the junior year groups. The delivery of Springboard is usually given to TAs, who need to receive appropriate training before they undertake this task. Some secondary schools, at least in Years 7 and 8, also draw on these catch-up programmes.

Difficulties presented by maths

Why is maths particularly difficult for some pupils?

Children may experience difficulties with any or all of the following:

- The variety of language and the number of alternative methods available to solve any one maths problem may cause confusion, but pupils need to know all of these methods, not least because they will be assessed on this knowledge in national exams.
- There may be too much for particular pupils to remember, particularly in mental maths.
- The speed or pace of the lesson may be too fast for some children and they get left behind; when this happens, it can be quite difficult to make sense of the next lessons, as the understanding of maths is cumulative – current knowledge builds upon previous knowledge.
- Keeping up with the NNS curriculum means that, for some pupils, there is not enough time for reinforcement of a particular topic; they may move on to a new topic before they have fully understood the current one.
- There may not be sufficient use of concrete, 'hands-on' materials to enable children to understand fully the concepts being taught; this may be particularly the case for visual and kinaesthetic learners (see page 32).
- Learning numerical facts by heart may not result in an understanding of the topic, with problems being encountered later on when what has been learnt by rote needs to be applied.
- Pupils may be able to do the calculation, but not have the language or vocabulary to explain the methods used or they need to take more time to organise thoughts.
- Where there are limited literacy skills, pupils may find they can do the maths itself, but they encounter difficulties because they cannot read the questions or write down their answers.
- Maths can provoke panic and panic causes the brain to 'shut down' or to react aggressively – *flight or fight mechanism* (see pages 95, 99–100).

Supporting pupils with special needs in maths

Role of the TA

All the principles which apply to the Literacy Hour apply to the Numeracy Hour. You can:

- help pupils understand what is being said by repeating it in simplified language;
- help pupils frame or formulate their own answers;
- remind pupils of what they have learnt previously;
- use visual stimuli and concrete apparatus such as games, number lines, multi-link;
- keep a pupil who is easily distracted focused on the lesson;
- help children write answers on whiteboards, scribing for those who find writing hard or laborious, or suggesting ideas which the pupils may like to consider;
- ensure that all pupils understand what is being asked of them and can read any materials that have been handed out;
- go over the teaching points made already in the lesson, taking time to give more explanation if that is needed;
- facilitate children working with each other by 'chairing' discussions;
- guide pupils in their own numeracy work;
- provide adapted resources when needed, including work in large print;
- work with pupils using ICT;
- prepare pupils to participate in the plenary;
- agree strategies with the teacher for including those children who find numeracy difficult.

(See also pages 94–6 on **dyscalculia**.)

Tips for supporting numeracy

Strategies for supporting numeracy are similar to those for supporting literacy. Essentially, this means using structured, cumulative and multi-sensory methods.

Not too much at once

It is better to teach a little, and ensure it is understood, than try and teach everything and end up with the pupil confused. During mental maths sessions, where the class is required to answer 10 or 20 questions within a certain time frame, you may be supporting pupils who need more time to process information. You could encourage them to try and answer every other question, giving them the opportunity to get at least half right, rather than seek to attempt all of them and, more than likely, get most or all of them wrong.

Make links and associations

Maths is all about links and associations, but often pupils do not see these links. You can support them by helping them appreciate the links. If, for instance, the pupils you are working with are being taught addition of tens and units, you can help them make associations with number bonds to 10, which they may already have learnt.

'Can you explain how you did this?'

Asking pupils to talk about how they approached certain problems or arrived at particular conclusions is an important element of TA support. It may be that, by listening to what they say, you can see why pupils are making errors and can teach to that gap or misunderstanding. Alternatively, pupils may have achieved the correct answer, but, through talking with them, you come to see that they have not fully understood how they came to that answer. Again, you can teach to this.

Ensure the basics are in place

As pupils get older and begin to evidence difficulties in maths, it is tempting to try and tackle the immediate presenting problem. This, in itself, may well be insufficient. You need to check that the pupil has a grasp of fundamental language such as 'bigger than, smaller than, first, second, after'. You also need to make sure that the pupil appreciates that sometimes different terminology means essentially the same thing; that, for example, 'subtraction,' 'difference' and 'minus' relate to essentially the same mathematical concept.

Misconceptions or misunderstandings can emerge when pupils are presented with fractions, percentages and decimals. A pupil may well seem to be able to calculate multiplication of whole numbers, but gets stumped with decimals. One reason may be an inadequate grasp of place value, or another may be that they have learnt that 'when you multiply by 10, add a nought' without understanding what that means and that it only applies to whole numbers.

Where you do discover gaps in basic knowledge, these gaps must be filled by effective teaching so that understanding can develop and be built upon. This, however, is easier said than done and you run into the same conflict as 'filling in the gaps' in literacy. If you withdraw pupils from lessons to teach basics, they miss out on the lesson content and are in danger of falling even further behind. If they stay in the lesson they may not understand what is going on and their sense of failure continues to be reinforced.

As a TA, if you do observe gaps in knowledge, you will need to discuss this with the teacher.

Use concrete apparatus

One resolution may be to use concrete, 'hands-on' apparatus. Whatever a pupil's abilities in maths, using concrete materials can effectively introduce or consolidate concepts. Using concrete apparatus involves more than giving pupils a number line or a number square. Both are useful, but they rely solely on visual skills; there is nothing tactile about them. More tactile equipment such as plastic or wooden cubes and rods is readily available in most primary schools. *Numicon* is an increasingly popular resource which provides apparatus to teach most of the Key Stage One numeracy curriculum, but can be used with pupils right into secondary school.

Use centimetre-squared paper

Using centimetre-squared paper, pupils are encouraged to write numerals in columns, which helps with pen and paper calculations. It helps pupils position their work correctly on the page and aids in the construction of shapes and graphs (see page 96).

Memory cards

Flashcards are always useful in maths and in literacy. Writing a number bond on one side of the card, with the answer on the reverse, can act as a useful aide-memoire and is something which can be taken home to learn. All the number bonds, multiplication tables, basic mathematical symbols and simple shapes can be written on memory cards. Such cards can also be used in small groups to play games like pairs, which can be a fun way to reinforce learning and may only take a few minutes.

Constant review

It is generally thought that a new piece of information takes 20 seconds to lodge in the short-term or 'working' memory, but needs 20 minutes to become secure in the long-term memory. Anything placed in the long-term memory needs to be consistently reviewed. As they say, 'Use it or lose it.'

This certainly applies to maths, and is especially significant as some mathematical concepts are only visited infrequently in the NNS. You can support pupils by ensuring that the concepts and facts they have been taught are reviewed regularly and frequently.

Using calculators

The use of calculators is an integral part of the numeracy syllabus and, rightly so, they can be very effective tools in the hands of those who know how to use them. But they should carry a 'numeracy health warning'. It is all too easy for pupils to become reliant on them, and they are no substitute for understanding basic mathematical calculations. Pupils who find numeracy difficult may well be tempted to use calculators to 'get the right answer', but using calculators in this way may conceal areas of misunderstanding. 'Getting the right answer' is not all there is to maths. Also, for pupils with areas of misunderstanding in maths, they may use a calculator inaccurately and not know they have done so.

In your support of pupils, therefore, by all means teach calculator skills, but do so with care.

Little and often

The key is 'little and often'. Ten minutes each day with individuals or a small group using memory cards, physical apparatus or whatever to reinforce, consolidate and generalise mathematical concepts and facts are far better than an hour each week of such activities. This may be hard to organise, but it is well worth it.

Checklist

✓ Mathematics presents particular difficulties to many pupils.
✓ Supporting pupils in maths necessitates discovering where the difficulties lie and addressing these issues.
✓ Strategies to support mathematical understanding should be structured, cumulative and multi-sensory.
✓ Emphasis should be given to developing understanding rather than simply 'working through the curriculum'.
✓ Helping pupils make links between mathematical concepts and encouraging them to talk through their thought processes is vital.
✓ A range of strategies are available to TAs to help pupils make progress in mathematics.

6 Tips for dealing with unacceptable behaviour

The school's behaviour policy – how the school responds to challenging behaviour

Take a collegiate approach

Every school will have a behaviour policy. This policy outlines the expectations the school has in regard to the behaviour of pupils. Pupils will have certain responsibilities. For example, pupils will listen to their teachers and carry out instructions as requested. In addition to responsibilities there will be consequences for not behaving in an appropriate fashion. The school policy will outline various levels of sanctions. The first course of action for dealing with a pupil who is not behaving as they should is to remind them of the rules. If the pupil continues to misbehave then perhaps a warning is given. If that does not seem to have the desired effect the pupil is kept in at playtime or a detention is given. For persistent misbehaviour the teacher will notify other relevant members of staff and parents.

A behaviour policy not only outlines what action is taken when a pupil misbehaves but also talks of what the school does to recognise and promote good behaviour. In schools rewards in the form of house points, stickers and merit points are given out. With regard to behaviour, it is often said that a school will take a collegiate approach to behaviour management. A collegiate approach implies that behaviour is everyone's responsibility.

Read the relevant policies

A TA needs to be familiar with the behaviour policy of the school. The school will also have policies on bullying, equal opportunities and issues relating to child protection and physical restraint (see page 15). Often the school secretary, teacher or SENCO will be able to provide the TA with copies of the necessary documents. As a TA you need to know what your role is within the policy and what the roles of other members of staff are.

You need to know what sanctions or rewards you as a TA can give out and what sanctions or rewards you need to discuss or negotiate with the teacher. For example, if pupils are not behaving as they should, what as a TA can you do? Can you remind the pupils of the rules? Can you talk to them about the consequences of not behaving appropriately? Can you insist that they stay in at playtime or have a detention *or* do you need to discuss this with the teacher? Likewise, if a pupil you are supporting has behaved well or has tried very hard, can you give out a sticker or a merit point *or* do you need to suggest this to the teacher? As a TA you will need to know what to do if you witness an incident of bullying, e.g. who do you report it to and what forms do you need to fill out?

Establish ground rules with the teacher you are working with

When working with a teacher, as well as knowing the behaviour policy, you will need to know the teacher's expectations for you and the pupils. A teacher will have expectations regarding the manner in which pupils come into the classroom, the level of background noise that is acceptable, where pupils should sit and who they should sit with. As a TA you can pass on this important information to any supply or cover teacher.

In addition a teacher will have certain expectations of a TA. Often TAs who are just starting to work with a teacher talk about their fear of over-stepping their role. For example, if the children are sitting on the carpet during Literacy Hour and one pupil is playing up, what as a TA can you do? Do you give them a 'look' and signal for them to be quiet? Do you move closer and sit next to them? Do you give them a verbal warning? Do you announce to the teacher that as such a pupil is not behaving you will take them to the back of the classroom? There are no right or wrong answers. How you support a teacher in dealing with disruptive behaviour in the class is a matter of negotiation. This means it is important to discuss with the teacher all aspects of your role.

Establish your authority with the pupils

Part of your role as a TA is knowing when to involve the teacher in disciplinary matters and when to try and resolve issues yourself. Again you will need to discuss these issues with the teacher. At one extreme a teacher would probably not be pleased if you brought every issue relating to behaviour to their attention (e.g. 'Sharon is not letting the other pupils have the dice'). A teacher requires the TA to establish their own authority with the pupils. For example, as a TA working with a pupil who is not sharing the 'dice' you could give the pupil choices. You could say to the pupil, 'if you do not share I will have to inform the teacher'. Sometimes this strategy is appropriate. However, you could also give the pupil a choice of either sharing or not participating in the game.

The school's policy on physical restraint

Find out about your school's policy on physical restraint

All LEAs will offer guidance to schools in this matter. As it stands, the law forbids a teacher from using any form of corporal punishment, to include any degree of physical contact that intends to punish a pupil by inflicting pain, injury or humiliation (see page 15). However, LEAs note that in extreme circumstances where the welfare and protection of pupils and staff are at risk, and as a last resort, reasonable and appropriate physical restraint may be used. As a TA you will need to become familiar with your school's policy on this issue.

Disclosures

Find out about your school's policy on disclosures

An important part of your job as a TA is to develop a relationship with the pupils you support. It is possible that in developing such a relationship a pupil confides in you. If this confidence involves abuse then, as a member of staff, you have a duty of care to the pupil to report what they say. For example, you might notice that a pupil you support seems angry and upset. You might ask them if anything is wrong. If they then tell you that they are upset because they lost their reading book and mummy got angry and kicked them in the stomach, that is a disclosure (see pages 16, 69, 88, 103).

The advice in such cases is:

- Listen to what the pupil has to say.
- Do not question them or prompt them.
- Remain calm when you listen to the details of the disclosure and do not communicate your shock to the pupil.
- Explain to the pupil that you are concerned for their well-being and that you cannot keep this information confidential but must report it to other members of staff.

Once you have informed the designated person (Child Protection Liaison Officer), you will then be asked to fill in records giving details regarding the disclosure. This information must be kept confidential (see page 16).

Behaviour support plans

Be familiar with the behavioural targets of the pupils you support

Pupils who have specific and persistent problems in behaviour will often have behaviour support plans or behavioural targets on IEPs (see pages 18–19). These targets should be specific (behaviour to be achieved should be described precisely), measurable (desired levels of behaviour will be stated), achievable (pupil should realistically be able to meet the target), relevant (targets personalised for individual pupil) and time limited (a set time is given for the pupil to reach the target). An example of a behavioural target could be 'to remain seated within a lesson', or 'to refrain from hitting other pupils'. The behaviour plan will not only outline the target to be achieved but describe possible resources, class strategies and specific techniques for the TA to use in helping the pupil to reach their target. If as a TA you are supporting a pupil who has behavioural targets then you will need to be familiar with the behavioural plan and you will need to feed back to the teacher and SENCO details regarding the pupil's progress.

DEALING WITH PUPILS WHO ARE:

Isolated and withdrawn

Be observant

There are many possible reasons for a pupil to be isolated and withdrawn. A pupil may have just started at a new school, could be having problems at home, could be being bullied or could lack social skills. Finding the reason behind the behaviour can help the school staff determine how best to help the individual pupil. If the pupil were having difficulties at home possibly due to parental divorce then maybe the pupil would benefit from pastoral support or counselling. If a pupil is isolated because they have difficulties in forming friends then social skills classes could help. As a TA you need to be observant. In formulating your observations consideration needs to be given to the following. Is the pupil isolated and withdrawn in all situations? Has this behaviour just started? Has the behaviour increased? What situations does the pupil find most difficult? What situations does the pupil find easier? Your observations need to be passed on to the teacher.

Be wary of over-dependence

A pupil who is isolated and withdrawn will need your support. Building a relationship with a pupil will take time. Techniques of active listening (see page 25) can help you achieve this. In a sense what you need to find out from the pupil is why they think they are isolated and what they think will help them to cope. A pupil who is isolated and withdrawn will need your encouragement. The danger for a TA in supporting a pupil who is isolated is that they can become over-dependent. If they are in the early years they may insist on always holding your hand at break time or always sitting besides you at circle time. In secondary school they may wait for you outside the staff room. This pupil may become very upset and angry when you are not at school. If you feel a pupil is becoming over-dependent on you this information needs to be communicated to other members of staff. As a TA you will need to talk to other staff about how to widen the support that this pupil has. Techniques such as **Circle of Friends** (see pages 87, 94) can be helpful when working with isolated and withdrawn pupils.

Attention seeking

Look to the underlying reasons

It would seem that a pupil who craves an audience and plays to the crowd is a very confident pupil. However, it could also be argued that a pupil who needs the attention of others actually has a low self-esteem (see pages 29–31). A pupil with low self-esteem needs constant approval and attention from others in order to feel good about themselves. In supporting a pupil who is attention seeking it is important to note how exactly a pupil seeks attention. Does calling attention to themselves involve putting other pupils down? Does calling attention to themselves involve having an argument, with the teacher or TA? Is this argument a way of establishing their 'street cred'? Is the pupil attention seeking in all situations? Does the pupil use attention-seeking devices, e.g. acting up and having an argument to avoid situations that they find difficult? A TA's observations on these matters needs to be communicated to the teacher.

If a pupil is using attention-seeking strategies to avoid a task that they find difficult, then consideration needs to be given to setting tasks that are achievable. If a pupil is attention-seeking due to a need to feel good then the TA needs to encourage and praise the pupil for appropriate behaviour.

Repeatedly calling out

Remind pupils of rules

A common problem in classrooms is the pupil who persistently calls out the answer without either raising their hands or waiting their turn. TAs often come across this difficulty when working with small groups. A first obvious point is to remind the pupils of rules regarding expected behaviour before starting to work with the group. Some pupils with specific difficulties, for instance ADHD (see pages 81–4), will find remembering to raise their hands when they want to talk difficult and will need to be reminded and encouraged to think before they call out. If such a pupil has their hand up but you cannot immediately respond to them, tell the pupil that you see them and assure them that it will be their turn soon. For pupils who have specific difficulties with this skill it is important for the TA to acknowledge how difficult the pupil finds this and to praise the pupil for trying to remember and for waiting their turn.

Distinguish between those who are eager to please and those who are deliberately disruptive

It is important for the TA to distinguish between pupils who call out, as they are thrilled that they know the answer and are eager to please, *and* those pupils who are being deliberately disruptive. The pupil who is eager to please will need constant reminders and praise both for their correct answers and for answering in the correct manner. The pupil who is being deliberately disruptive will need firmer handling. However, you will need to be clear to the pupil who is deliberately disruptive why you are taking a firm approach with them and not with others. In such a discussion it is helpful to try and appeal to the pupil's better nature and to recognise their potential. For example, you could say, 'I am depending on you to set an example to the others'. If this does not work a discussion regarding the consequences of not behaving appropriately is needed. Tell the pupil that they have a choice: either they behave correctly or they face the consequences for not behaving. Stress that the choice is up to them. Remember, important and sensitive discussions such as these are best said in private.

Over-cautious and unsure

Need for praise and encouragement

A pupil who is over-cautious and unsure will be hesitant at taking on new tasks. This pupil will hate to make mistakes. This pupil will not answer a question in class. The fear of not being able to do a task, the fear of making a mistake, is preventing this pupil from achieving their potential.

A TA can work with this pupil by encouraging them gradually to try more and more. At times a TA might ask the pupil what they think the answer is; then, if the answer is correct, the TA can encourage the pupil to put their hand up. You could have an arrangement with the teacher that when you give a signal the teacher will ask your pupil for the answer.

Help the pupil to see that making mistakes is part of the learning process

A pupil who is over-cautious will need much praise and encouragement to boost their self-esteem (see pages 29–31), but at the same time it is important to talk with the pupil about how they feel when they make a mistake. The reality of life is that we all make mistakes and that often we actually learn more from our mistakes than from when things go to plan. Sometimes it is helpful to talk to the pupils about how you feel when you make a mistake and how you have learned from mistakes. The lesson to learn is that even when you make a mistake it is important not to give up.

Always copying from others

Use questions to assess understanding

As a TA you are there to help the pupils learn. Your role is to ensure not only that the pupil has the correct information written in their textbook or worksheet, but also that they understand what they have written. One way to check understanding is to question the pupil about their work. In your feedback to the teacher, the teacher wants to hear details both of what pupils have completed and what they have understood. A pupil who passively copies down the answers either from other pupils or from the board is not learning.

Find out the reasons behind their copying behaviour

There could be many reasons why a pupil is copying the answers from others. Perhaps the pupil has just not understood but does not want to admit that they are lost. Perhaps the pupil feels that they will be told off if they say that they do not understand. It is much easier for the pupil to copy the answers than to have to tell the teacher or TA that they have no idea about what is going on. This is especially true if a pupil feels that all the other pupils do understand. Your role in supporting pupils is to assure them that it is *all right* not to understand. Once you have established what the pupil knows or doesn't know, then you can work with them to expand their knowledge.

From a different perspective, sometimes a pupil will have difficulties copying material from the board or the textbook. A pupil could have difficulties seeing the board. A pupil could have difficulties in handwriting. In these cases the work that the pupil is set may need to be altered in some way. Perhaps the pupil needs a copy of the on-board notes besides them. Perhaps as a TA you will need to scribe for them.

Defensive

Need to boost self-esteem

There are occasions when you will come across a pupil who is defensive, who seems to have a chip on their shoulder. This pupil not only has difficulties in accepting criticism but also interprets ordinary comments as criticisms. This is the pupil who believes that everyone is having a go at them. Often this defensiveness is an indicator of a low self-esteem. This pupil needs praise and encouragement to boost self-esteem (see pages 29–31).

A gentle approach is needed, because, to begin with, this pupil might not accept the praise for what it is but see it as sarcasm. Remember that praise to be effective must be genuine.

A pupil who is defensive needs help in recognising their strong points. A pupil who is defensive needs help in listening skills. They need actually to listen to what others are saying rather than to what they think others are saying. Asking the pupil to repeat what has been said to them can be useful as it can highlight misunderstandings. Special input in the form of social skills can also help.

Immature

Look out for immature behaviour

Though schools focus on teaching skills such as reading, writing and mathematics, the social aspects of school, such as developing friendships, learning how to stand up for oneself and how to get on with all sorts of individuals are equally important. As a TA you will need to look out for pupils who seem immature for their age. Pupils who are immature may not be able to cope with pupils of their own age and prefer to interact and play with pupils several years younger. Their peers often see pupils who are labelled immature as babyish, in that they have mannerisms or prefer activities that many of their peers have grown out of: for example, an 8-year-old boy who still sucks his thumb when upset, or a 14-year-old girl who still likes to play with dolls. All children will mature at different rates, but a child who is very different from their peers will likely have problems in establishing age-appropriate friendships.

There can be many reasons for immature behaviour. Sometimes immature behaviour might be a result of some trauma or difficulty that the pupil has experienced, e.g. divorce, being placed in foster care (see pages 16, 46, 103). Such a pupil would benefit from pastoral support or, in extreme cases, professional counselling. Sometimes, placing the pupil near other pupils who are known to be kind and supportive is useful.

Encourage age-appropriate behaviour

Sometimes a pupil who is displaying seemingly immature behaviour is doing so because they have not learned how to behave appropriately. Individuals with **Asperger's syndrome** (see pages 85–8) will have great difficulties in learning the social rules of behaviour that many of us take for granted. Social skills classes where skills such as how to take turns, how to have a conversation, how close to stand to someone when you are talking, can be helpful.

Some pupils who behave in an immature manner may do so because they may be rewarded for such behaviour by receiving lots of attention, e.g. the youngest child in the family who gets a lot of attention for acting as the baby. Some pupils with **Down's syndrome** may act inappropriately owing to low expectations from others (see pages 92–4). In such cases the pupil in question needs to be given attention and praise for acting in a more age-appropriate manner.

Insecure

Try to identify the underlying reasons

Insecurity can be caused by a number of factors, a change of circumstances such as a move to a new school or changes in the family, e.g. a divorce, the birth of a new brother or sister.

It is important to distinguish between pupils who have always had a tendency to be insecure and those who suddenly seem to lose their confidence. If you notice that a previously confident pupil is not coping then this information needs to be passed on to the teacher. A conversation with a parent might reveal family problems such as a bereavement or divorce that will need to be taken into consideration.

Routines can help

Some pupils, particularly pupils on the autistic spectrum (see pages 85–8), will appear insecure when placed in a new environment, as they will find changes in routine extremely difficult. If possible try to keep to routines. If there is to be a change in routines it is helpful to warn the pupil of the change beforehand. For example, if you always support a pupil in class but you know that next week you are to go on a training day, then it is advisable that you discuss this with the pupil you are supporting.

Reassure and encourage

As a TA there is much that you can do to reassure pupils that you are there for them. To begin with, emphasise to the pupil that it is normal for everyone to feel insecure at times. Be there to support them. Encourage the pupil to ask others for support. Try to build their confidence by giving them responsibility. As a TA you are there to support pupils, but look out for the pupil becoming over-dependent on you. Your ultimate goal is not for the pupil to find security in you but for the pupil to find security in their beliefs that they can deal with the changes that life brings.

The class clown

Look for the underlying reasons

The class clown is always an interesting character and can add an element of fun to the class. The class clown can be amusing, but not so amusing when you find that you are not covering all the work that you should be. If you have the class clown in your group you will need to communicate to this pupil that there is a time and place for jokes and there is a time and place for getting down to work.

It is also important to look for reasons for the behaviour. Does the pupil just have a wicked sense of humour? Is the pupil using humour, making jokes as a way of getting attention? Is the pupil using humour to put other pupils down? Is the clown a very able pupil who is bored by what they are being asked to do, or is the clown a less able pupil who is using humour as a way to avoid doing what they should be doing?

If the pupil is constantly playing to the crowd, or using jokes to put others down, then maybe there is an underlying issue of low self-esteem (see pages 29–31). Perhaps you will need to praise the pupil for doing their work, or participating appropriately in group or class discussions.

Play your role in setting appropriate tasks

If the pupil is using humour as a means of escaping either very boring or extremely difficult work then you will need to have a word with the teacher regarding setting more suitable tasks. If the set task meets the ability level of the pupil then perhaps the pupil will not need to act the clown.

Continuously questioning everything

Ensure that all pupils you are working with understand the questions

Asking questions is an essential part of the learning process. However, there are times when a pupil asking questions can present problems. Sometimes you will come across a pupil who just loves to ask questions. Sometimes this pupil happens to be a very able pupil and asks very interesting and informed questions. The danger in working with a class, or a group, which has one exceptionally able pupil is that if you are not careful you could end up teaching to that one pupil, rather than meeting the needs of the group. There are times when a question might need to be rephrased so that all the pupils you are working with understand it. At times, rather than answer the question yourself, it is useful to ask other pupils' opinions.

Look to underlying reasons

There are times when you might feel that the pupil is asking questions but that the questions have nothing to do with what you are supposed to be working on. If this is the case then perhaps the pupil is using questions as a way of avoiding a task that they feel unable to do. If you feel that the set work is not appropriate for the pupil you might need to adapt the task so that it is appropriate or ask the teacher for alternative work.

Set ground rules for asking questions

Before beginning group work it is useful to set ground rules for questions. As a TA you want to encourage the group to ask questions but you need to remind them that the questions need to be about what you are discussing. If the pupil asks a question that is not completely on topic, answer the question. But also try to rephrase the question so that it becomes relevant to what you should be talking about.

Be honest – admit that you do not always know the answer

Another issue that concerns TAs is what to do if a pupil asks a question that you do not know the answer to. This can happen particularly at secondary school level. It is important to be honest with the pupil. Tell the pupil that you do not know the answer. Sometimes you may need to ask the teacher for guidance. Sometimes you could ask a more able pupil to help you and the pupil you are supporting. Sometimes you can ask the pupil how they think you can find the answer. Would looking in a textbook, on the Internet or in a dictionary be helpful? Pupils find it comforting that you too find the questions difficult. Learning is not about already knowing the answers but learning how to discover the answers.

Limited in their attention span

Help the pupil to start the task

Some pupils will have difficulties in getting down to work and staying focused on the task in hand. Some pupils will have specific conditions, e.g. ADHD (see pages 81–4), that will make paying attention difficult. The first point to make when supporting a pupil with a short attention span is to ensure that they know what the task is that they should be doing. Often if the pupil has not been paying attention they have no idea about what they should be doing. Have the pupil tell you what they should be doing. Help the pupil start the task. Sometimes writing down what the pupil should be doing can serve as a useful reminder.

Talk to the teacher about what are realistic targets for the pupil. Appreciate how difficult it is for the pupil to concentrate. Working in short bursts is sometimes helpful. Praise the pupil for their effort. Gradually increase your expectations for the pupil.

Taking a long time to respond

Recognise the reflective pupil

As discussed in learning styles (see pages 31–5), individuals differ in how they process and take in information. Some pupils are reflective, they do not like to be rushed, they like to think before speaking or writing their answers down. It is important for teachers and TAs to realise that individual pupils have different learning styles. However, it is also important for pupils to recognise that they each have different ways of learning. What you do not want is for the pupil who does like to take time to reflect to be teased for doing that.

If you are working with a group of pupils where you know one pupil likes to think before responding then give them time to formulate an answer in their mind. Tell the group what the question is and give them all time to think about the answer. Ask your reflective pupil for their contribution last.

It is important to distinguish between the pupil who takes a long time to respond, as they are reflective, and the pupil who is over-cautious and unsure (see pages 71–2).

Telling lies repeatedly

Be observant

Here as a TA you need to be observant. You need to pay attention to the types of lies the pupils is saying. Does the pupil lie to avoid getting in trouble? Does the pupil tell outrageous lies to draw attention to themselves? Does the pupil actually believe what they say is true? All these observations need to be passed on to the teacher or SENCO. Telling lies repeatedly could be an indicator of low self-esteem or a way of coping with personal difficulties.

Pupils who are being bullied

Look out for signs of bullying

Every school will have a policy on bullying (see page 14). As a TA you will need to be familiar with this policy. Bullying is usually not a one-off incident but a persistent pattern of behaviour that inflicts harm on a victim. Bullying can take many forms. It can be physical, e.g. the pupil who is beaten up. It can involve the threat of physical harm. It can be emotional in nature, name calling, being excluded from activities, and receiving hurtful text messages or e-mails.

Most bullying policies will state that the school expects pupils to act towards each other in a relationship of mutual respect, that the school will treat all incidents of bullying seriously and that all pupils are encouraged to approach staff with any problems they might have. The difficulty with bullying is that often the victim may be reluctant to tell staff. There are many reasons for this. Perhaps they feel that if they tell it will only make matters worse. Perhaps they feel ashamed and feel that they are somehow to blame for what is happening. As such a TA needs to be observant.

A TA needs to look for indicators of possible bullying. A pupil may be socially isolated. The pupil may always sit by themselves at lunch- or break times. They might be the pupil that no one else wants in their group. This pupil might appear angry or tearful. The pupil will lack confidence and be clearly unhappy. There may be a sudden change in behaviour, i.e. a previously confident and able pupil who no longer seems to care. A pupil who is being bullied may be constantly teased by other pupils. The other pupils may say this is only a bit of fun, but such a situation requires further investigation. As a TA you could ask other pupils about what is happening. Incidents of bullying need to be reported. The victim needs to be encouraged to talk about what is happening.

A pupil who is being bullied will have low self-esteem. As a TA you will need to work with the pupil in ways that will raise their self-esteem (see pages 29–31).

Helping to change the behaviour of bullies

Find out about the approaches your school uses to handle bullying

If bullying is to be stopped the behaviour of the bully needs to be tackled. Often a pupil who bullies others has an underlying difficulty that needs to be dealt with. A bully, though it might not seem so, is often lacking in self-esteem. Putting others down makes them feel good and powerful. Often a pupil who is a bully has been the victim of bullying. As such, many schools will have programmes that deal with both the bully and the victim. Some schools will have a 'no-blame approach' to bullying. This approach, rather than focusing on punishing the bully, focuses on solving the problem. Other programmes include peer mentoring and peer mediation. Talk to the teacher or SENCO and find out about the approaches that your school uses to deal with bullies.

As a TA you will need to work with those pupils that are bullying in order to raise their self-esteem. With this pupil you will need to make a clear distinction between their behaviour and the person that they are. The behaviour was wrong but they are still potentially a good person.

Restoring and rebuilding relationships with pupils

Be familiar with your school's strategies in this area

Pupils who seriously misbehave will at times be excluded from school. However, at some point these pupils will be back in the classroom. On a less dramatic note, you will at times have very difficult days with pupils. Things might be said in the heat of the moment. But again you will find yourself working with these same pupils the next day.

Schools often talk about repair and rebuild strategies. Imagine that a pupil has seriously hurt another pupil. You, as a witness to the event, were extremely angry with that pupil. To move forward the pupil will need a chance to explore the reasons for their behaviour and also to make amends. As a TA you will need to work to restore your relationship with this pupil. You will need to make a distinction between the behaviour and the person. You will need to see the potential in the pupil and work with the pupil so that they can see their potential.

At times you might say things to a pupil that you later regret; if this is the case you will need to apologise. As part of rebuilding your relationship with the pupil it is helpful to make a point of praising the pupil when they are behaving in an appropriate manner – the 'catch them when they are good' approach.

Checklist

✓   Read and familiarise yourself with the relevant policies.
✓   Talk to other staff regarding your specific role in managing behaviour.
✓   Know the behaviour targets for the pupils you support.
✓   Inform other staff if you notice any worrisome behaviour.
✓   Look for the underlying reasons for behaviour.
✓   Praise pupils for appropriate behaviour.

7 Tips for TAs for supporting pupils with special needs

A part of a TA's role is to understand specialist terminology, as follows in alphabetical order.

ADHD (Attention Deficit Hyperactivity Disorder)

A pupil who has problems in maintaining attention will often seem to have their 'head in the clouds'. This pupil will make careless mistakes in written work as they have not read or listened to the instructions. Such a pupil will have difficulty staying on task, will be easily distracted and will often fail to finish set work. This pupil has problems with organisation, will often turn up late to class and arrive without the proper equipment.

A pupil who is hyperactive will have difficulty keeping still. This pupil will be constantly fidgeting. A pupil who is hyperactive may have a need to rock constantly back and forth on their chair or drum on their desk. This pupil, though instructed to stay in their seat, may find it impossible to do so.

A pupil who is impulsive will act first and think later. This is the type of pupil who would hit a fellow pupil, if provoked, without thinking of the consequences. This is the type of pupil who might climb onto the roof of the school to sunbathe without considering the appropriateness or the personal dangers involved in such an act.

Though this condition is characterised by hyperactivity, impulsivity and problems in maintaining attention, the secondary effects are said to be difficulties in maintaining relationships with peers and the potential for problems with low self-esteem (see pages 29–31). A pupil who has problems listening and acts without thinking will often find themselves in trouble at school. A pupil who constantly drums on their desk and barges in on others' conversations or games will annoy other members of their class. Being in trouble at school and having difficulties in getting on with other pupils can have an impact on self-esteem *if* the pupil starts to believe that they are no good and that no one likes them.

A TA will need to take all these factors into consideration when dealing with such pupils.

Try to see the world from the pupil's perspective

Be aware of what factors the pupil would find distracting. Perhaps sitting by the window overlooking the school's busy car park with people coming and going is not a good idea. Make the pupil aware that you know that they find focusing and staying on task difficult. Praise them for their efforts towards staying focused. Their powers of concentration may not match those of the other pupils in class but recognise and reward small steps in the right direction.

Talk to the teacher about who works best together

Think about who the pupil would work best with. Ideally they would need to sit with pupils who would not distract them, as well as pupils who would not be distracted by them. Ideally these pupils would be able and willing to offer assistance to the pupil if they were having difficulties in understanding their work. Ideally these pupils would serve as good role models for how to behave within a class. Obviously these are factors that the teacher will take into consideration when drawing up a seating plan. It is important to talk to the teacher concerning your opinions and observations about which pupils work well together and equally what seating combinations would be a disaster waiting to happen.

Ensure that the pupil knows what is expected of them

Sometimes a pupil may not be doing what they should be doing because they simply were not paying attention when the instructions were given. Check that the pupil knows what the task is. Ensure that the pupil knows what they have to do to complete the task. Have them repeat the instructions back to you to check for understanding. Make sure that the pupil has the skills to do the task. Tasks set should be achievable. Talk about what they should do if they get stuck. Tell them that they have the option to put their hands up and someone will help them or suggest another pupil they might go to for support. Assure them that, if they need help, you will be back but that they must wait patiently. If you see them with their hands up, either verbally or non-verbally let them know that you have seen them and that you will get to them as soon as possible.

Help the pupil with organisation skills

Some TAs working in large and busy secondary schools state that they meet the pupils they support briefly at the beginning of the day to ensure that the pupils have all the equipment that they need and that they know what they are doing on that particular day. Most TAs will have with them a collection of extra pencils and equipment that pupils can borrow if necessary. As pupils progress through the school system, homework becomes increasingly more important. A TA can assist a pupil with ADHD by ensuring that they have filled in their homework diary appropriately.

Having clear expectations about rules and behaviour for all pupils will help pupils with ADHD.

Specific routines and clear expectations of behaviour will help ADHD pupils to know their boundaries. It is important that you remind pupils of class expectations. For example, you could say:

> Now, for this part of the class you are sitting in Red group and when we are sitting in this group you will need to have your writing book and dictionary out. If you need to leave the group or wish to ask a question you need to put your hand up.

Sometimes rules and expectations need to be restated every time you start to work with a group.

Try alternative strategies to help the pupil to focus

If a pupil finds it very difficult to listen to the teacher without fidgeting it is sometimes helpful for the pupil to have something specific to do or fidget with. This strategy will always need to be talked through with the teacher. If a child finds it impossible to sit on the carpet and listen to the teacher during the Numeracy or Literacy Hour perhaps having a small object to hold on to (e.g. a squidgy ball) will prevent the child from poking the pupils they sit beside. As the saying goes, 'the devil makes work for idle thumbs'. If a pupil in a secondary school cannot listen to the teacher without drumming on their desk, then perhaps being given a spare piece of paper and being allowed to doodle will help them to keep still and quiet. This strategy will let them and others around them focus on what the teacher is saying.

Encourage pupils with ADHD to think before they act

As stated, one characteristic of ADHD is impulsivity. Pupils need to be taught strategies to help them deal with this aspect. Pupils need to be encouraged to think before they act. For example, pupils could be instructed and reminded to 'count to 10' before acting. While they are 'counting to 10' they need to think about the possible consequences of their planned action. Of course another tactic would be to be aware of possible temptations and potentially dangerous situations. Placing pupils with ADHD next to electrical sockets and windows that could open is not a good idea.

The use of medication

Many pupils with ADHD will be prescribed medication. The most common medication is Ritalin (methylphenidate), a short-acting medication. The effects of Ritalin begin to kick in 20 to 40 minutes after administration with maximum effectiveness occurring after an hour and a half. However, Ritalin begins to wear off after four hours. Therefore a pupil on Ritalin will need to take the medication more than once a day. It is common for a pupil to take Ritalin in the morning and then at lunch. The prescribed use of Ritalin is controversial. Those in favour of the drug state evidence that it has been found to improve attention and impulse control and decrease incidences of hyperactivity in 70–90 per cent of children with ADHD (Barkley, 1998). However, even the strongest supporters of the drug will say that at best it provides 'a window of opportunity', allowing the pupil to be open to strategies as described above.

Allergies

An allergy is the body's negative response to a substance. For many individuals this substance may be totally harmless. But to someone who is allergic to it the substance will be treated as an invading organism by their immune system. Many individuals are allergic to household dust mites or pollen in the air. The allergic reactions to this substance could range from comparatively minor symptoms, e.g. runny nose, sneezing or mild eczema, to a potentially fatal anaphylactic shock. Anaphylaxis or anaphylactic shock is a severe allergic reaction, which can be fatal within minutes. This reaction involves the swelling of the airways, a dramatic drop in blood pressure and loss of consciousness. Some individuals will have severe allergic reactions to certain foods (e.g. peanuts), medications, insect bites or latex. Those individuals with a history of severe allergic reactions will be prescribed self-injectable epinephrine or EpiPen. For an individual with a severe allergic reaction, the immediate injection of epinephrine can mean the difference between life and death. As a TA you will need to know if any of the pupils you support have severe allergies. If they do, you will need to know what the pupil is allergic to, the symptoms of the allergy, if necessary where to locate medication and how to administer it (see page 15).

Asthma

Be familiar with the school's policy on asthma

Asthma is a common medical condition. It is likely that several children within each class will have this condition. Asthma affects the airways, i.e. the small tubes that carry air in and out of the lungs. The airways of individuals with asthma are almost always inflamed. This condition is made worse if the individual has a cold or infection or comes in contact with something from the environment that triggers asthma. Examples of environmental triggers are pollen, cigarette smoke and household dust mites. Stress and laughter can also bring on an asthma attack in some individuals.

Though many people have asthma, the degree to which an individual will have asthma will vary. Further, each individual will have their own unique triggers that seem to bring on the condition.

The symptoms of asthma include coughing, wheezing, a shortness of breath and a tight chest. When an individual has all of these symptoms that individual is having an asthma attack. At this point the individual will need to take medication, in the form of an inhaler. Reliever inhalers are used whenever asthma symptoms develop. Pupils who have asthma within a school will need to keep these inhalers close at hand. Each school will have a school policy regarding asthma. As a TA you should become familiar with this policy and make sure that you know the pupils within your school who have asthma and the procedures to take should they have an asthma attack at school (Asthma UK, 2002) (see page 15).

Autistic spectrum disorder

Autistic spectrum disorder, or ASD as it is known, refers to individuals who have difficulties with social interactions, problems in communication and imaginative activity and a limited range of activities and interests. As a TA what you will notice in terms of difficulties with social interactions is that the pupil has a reluctance to maintain eye contact, that they have difficulties in understanding body language and facial expressions, that they do not have age-appropriate friendships, that they lack empathy and have difficulties in understanding and responding to emotions. In terms of language, individuals with ASD will either have very limited language or use language in unusual ways. Some pupils will have difficulties in making conversations. Such pupils will often break social rules, e.g. asking the headmistress why her hair is going grey. Pupils with ASD will take what you say literally. So if you say 'Hang on', they might reply 'hang on to what?' One of the main indicators of ASD is lack of spontaneous make-believe play. In addition individuals with ASD will have a preoccupation with restricted areas of interests that is said to be unusual in its intensity or focus. For example, a pupil may become fascinated with bus timetables, or have a passion for lawn mowers.

ASD is said to be a continuum in that individuals with this condition will differ greatly in terms of ability. At one end you may have a pupil with severe learning disabilities and no language, while at the other end you may have a very bright pupil, gifted in maths but with absolutely no social skills and a difficulty in making friends.

There has been much debate about whether Asperger's syndrome refers to individuals at the more able end of the autistic spectrum or whether it is a unique condition in its own right. Individuals with Asperger's will have difficulties in social interactions and understanding the social meanings involved in language and communication (**semantic pragmatic disorder**).

Give consideration to how you are communicating

Pupils with ASD can be reluctant to engage in eye contact; do not expect this and never force a pupil to maintain eye contact.

As stated, pupils with ASD will have difficulties with language or social communication. For pupils with no language, advice needs to be sought from speech therapists. For pupils with difficulties in taking speech literally, consideration needs to be given to what is said. A TA will need to avoid sayings such as 'It is raining cats and dogs' or that the 'Christmas holidays seemed like a month of Sundays'. A pupil with ASD does not read between the lines. The meaning of the question 'Were you born in a barn?' would be lost on them. Therefore communication needs to be clear and specific, e.g. 'Can you please remember to close the door?' Likewise, when asking pupils to complete tasks it is important that you give clear instructions. Comments such as 'Have a go' are not really helpful. Instructions such as 'Sit down at your desk. Read over the addition problems on the worksheet and then answer all the addition questions on the page' are much clearer.

Where possible put in place routines and warn the pupil in advance of any changes to routines

A pupil with ASD likes routines. Being able to predict what is going to happen to them, and when, makes them feel safe. When pupils feel safe then they can get down to the business of learning. Therefore, having predictable routines is important. Timetables are important. **Visual timetables** are useful with pupils who have limited language. Sometimes, having visual aids such as a very large egg timer is helpful with pupils who cannot read the time, because the aids can be used to indicate when it is time to move on to the next activity.

Though routines are important, the reality is that in a busy school things do not always go to plan. Therefore it is helpful for the TA to pre-warn pupils of impending changes to plans. A useful strategy with able pupils is to work on the concept of 'usually' and 'sometimes', meaning that most of the time we will try to follow the routines but there are times when this will not be possible.

Use areas of interest to enhance the learning process

Pupils with ASD will often have areas of interest that are unusual in intensity and focus. However, such interests can be used creatively. Time spent looking at a book on lawn mowers can be used as a reward for completing a maths worksheet. Another strategy is to adapt the set work to include the pupils' particular interests. A maths worksheet focusing on simple addition could be modified to involve the addition of lawn mowers.

Support friendships

Pupils with ASD will have difficulties with friendships; in fact a lack of friendships is one of the defining features of Asperger's. Often pupils with Asperger's will be desperate to have friends – it is just that they don't seem to know how to go about it. Here programmes such as Circle of Friends (see pages 70, 94), where a group of classmates volunteer to support and befriend the pupil with ASD, are very useful. Talk to the teacher or SENCO regarding specific interventions.

Be sensitive to situations that might prove overwhelming

Pupils with ASD will find school, due to its unpredictability, a very overwhelming place. In addition, pupils with ASD might suffer from sensory overload. Some individuals with ASD will process sensory information, i.e. sights, sounds, touch, smell, in different ways. For example, one pupil could make all the noise they like, but experience other children's cries as painful. Be aware of the possibility of sensory overload. Talk to the teacher about having a place where the pupil with ASD can go if it all appears to be too much. Know the pupil you are working with and pick up on the signals that indicate that the pupil is having difficulties. Intervene early to avoid the situation getting out of control. Better still, with more able pupils, offer them a way (e.g. giving you a red card) whereby they can tell you that they need time out.

Find out as much as you can

There are many specialist programmes that have been seen to be effective with pupils with ASD. Talk to the teacher, SENCO and other TAs, who will have valuable information to share.

Depression

Look out for signs of depression and pass on your concerns

It has often been thought that depression is something that happens to adults. However, children can suffer from depression too. As a TA it is part of your role to look out for unusual or worrying patterns of behaviour and refer these to the teacher. A pupil with depression will need support. Some schools will have a designated member of staff who can offer pastoral support or counselling. Sometimes a pupil will need to be referred to mental health services.

Depression can be triggered by external factors such as bereavement, divorce or sexual abuse. As a TA you will over time come to have a relationship with the pupils you support. A pupil might disclose very personal and disturbing details. At this point you will need to follow the school's procedures regarding disclosures (see pages 16, 68, 69, 103). Though the pupil might ask you to treat the information as confidential, you will need to tell the pupil that as a member of staff you have a duty of care to report the matter.

A pupil with depression:

- May talk of feeling unhappy, miserable and lonely or in extreme cases of wanting to die.
- May talk of feeling guilty. They may blame themselves, e.g. 'It is all my fault.' They may say they hate themselves.
- May be moody, tearful, irritable and easily upset.
- May start to avoid friends and stop participating in school activities that they used to enjoy.
- May stop looking after themselves. They may no longer pay attention to their appearance. They may stop eating.
- They may appear tired at school and find it difficult to concentrate

A pupil with depression may not necessarily have all of these signs, but any of these signs do need to be reported to a teacher. Professional advice needs to be sought.

Developmental coordination disorders/dyspraxia

These conditions, also known as dyspraxia (see page 57), apply to individuals who have difficulties in motor coordination, specifically both gross and fine motor skills. Gross motor skills refer to large movements involved in running and skipping, while fine motor skills involve the specialised movements needed to write or use a pair of scissors. In the past individuals with this condition were often labelled as clumsy. In addition, some individuals with this disorder will have difficulties with the motor movements involved in speech.

A TA will notice that a pupil with this condition has messy handwriting. This pupil will have difficulties in getting dressed and undressed for PE. This pupil will invariably be the last one ready. This pupil will find it difficult to participate in PE activities that their fellow pupils enjoy and will drop and bump into things. This pupil will have a poor auditory short-term memory, i.e. they will find it difficult to remember what you have just said to them. In addition, the pupil may have a poor visual memory, making copying from the board difficult. This pupil will have poor organisation skills and will often come to lesson unprepared as they have forgotten what to bring. With all these difficulties this pupil will often have low self-esteem.

Find out more about special programmes

Pupils with this disorder will benefit greatly from specialised programmes designed to improve gross and fine motor skills. Often schools will get advice for such programmes from physiotherapists. Programmes such as **brain-gym** or hand-gym (see page 57) can be effective. Your teacher and SENCO will have valuable information on these programmes.

Make sure that set tasks are achievable

Set tasks need to be achievable. Never ask the pupil to do a task that you know they cannot do. For example, 'Can you go to the back of the classroom and bring me that pile of textbooks from the third shelf?' This is a case for getting to know the strengths and limitations of the pupils you support. When you ask the pupil to do a task, ask them to do something that they can succeed at, e.g. 'Can you give this book to the teacher for me?' When the pupil succeeds, praise them. Pupils with this condition need lots of praise to boost their self-esteem.

It is important that work set for this pupil is realistic. As the pupil will have difficulties in writing, they will take longer to complete work;

therefore shorter tasks may be necessary. Talk to the teacher regarding what are realistic targets and if you feel that the set work is too much for the pupil to complete. The teacher will value your feedback.

Work with the teacher in order to make PE a pleasurable experience

PE is one lesson that a pupil with developmental coordination disorders will find difficult. The difficulties begin with getting dressed. It is possible that the pupil, especially younger pupils, may need help in learning how to get dressed and undressed. Such techniques could be discussed and practised at a suitable time and place. Perhaps extra time could be given for dressing and undressing. Perhaps you could encourage a friend to act as a buddy and help the pupil if necessary.

When it comes to participating in games avoid situations where pupils get to choose who is on their team. Being the last pupil chosen is always a blow to self-esteem. Where possible try to differentiate the activity so that the pupil can achieve. If pupils are put in pairs try to think of someone who would be supportive. The teacher would value your suggestions with regard to supportive friends or ideas on how activities could be adapted.

Be aware of problems with visual memory

As stated, pupils can have poor visual memory. Having a poor visual memory will mean that they have difficulties in copying from the board. If working in a small group you might find that using different coloured pens when writing on a whiteboard helpful as it makes individual sentences or words stand out. Sometimes it is helpful if the pupil has beside them a copy of the work that is written on the board.

Implement appropriate strategies to assist handwriting

Handwriting (see page 57) is an area which will cause the pupil great difficulties because it involves the use of very skilled and refined movements. In addition, handwriting involves visual memory and perceptual skills. Such memory and perceptual skills are needed to recognise the difference between shapes, to keep the letters on a line and to get the correct spacing between letters and words.

A TA can help by being aware of how difficult the task is for a pupil with this condition and allowing extra time. It is important that TAs reward effort and recognise and celebrate small achievements.

In the early years of schooling a TA can concentrate on ensuring that the pupil's pencil hold is the correct 'dynamic tripod grip' (see pages 58–9). That is, the pencil is grasped between the pads of the index finger and thumb and that the pencil rests comfortably on the side of the middle finger. Once bad habits or inefficient ways of holding a pencil are learnt, then it becomes not impossible but more difficult to teach the pupil the correct grip. There are a variety of writing tools which include pencil grips that can be used. However, these modifications, in order to improve hand-writing, will need to be used correctly by the pupil. As a TA you will need to ensure that the pupil is using the modification correctly. Here you will need to talk to your teacher or SENCO for guidance.

For pupils who find it difficult to keep letters on the line, different sizes of lined paper can be useful. For number work, squared graph paper of a suitable size can be used in order to ensure that numbers are laid out correctly. In order to write effectively the paper is usually kept in position by the non-writing hand. Again pupils might have difficulties with this. Sometimes, taping or attaching the paper to the writing surface with Blu-Tack is helpful. However, the paper will need to be adjusted as the pupil reaches the bottom of the page.

Another common difficulty with writing is learning how much pressure to apply to the page. One way of practising the correct amount of pressure to apply involves games with carbon paper. Putting layers of carbon paper and additional paper underneath the writing page allows the pupil to prac-tise the correct amount of pressure. If their marks on the writing page go through the carbon paper to the pages underneath, this indicates that they are using too much pressure.

One factor often overlooked in writing is that the pupil must be comfortably seated. The furniture should be the correct size for the pupil. A child, in order to write effectively, needs to be able to sit with feet flat on the floor and knees free of the underside of the table.

Diabetes

Diabetes is a condition in which the amount of glucose (sugar) in the blood is too high. Insulin, a hormone made in the pancreas, normally controls the level of glucose within the blood. Most children with diabetes will have Type 1 Diabetes, meaning that their bodies do not produce insulin. Diabetes cannot be cured but it can be treated. Treatment in children involves insulin injections and appropriate diet. Insulin cannot be taken by mouth, like many other medications, as the stomach juices would destroy it. Therefore it needs to be injected. The aim of treatment is to keep blood sugar levels within a normal range, not too high (hyperglycaemia) and not too low (hypoglycaemia). The most common short-term complication of diabetes is hypoglycaemia, when blood sugar levels fall too low. As a TA you will need to know if any of the pupils whom you are supporting have diabetes. You will need to take advice about how to notice if a pupil's blood sugar levels are too low and advice about the immediate action to be taken. (Diabetes UK, 2003) (see page 14).

Down's syndrome

Down's syndrome (see page 74) is the result of a chromosome disorder where instead of there being 46 chromosomes in each cell there are 47. Down's individuals have an extra chromosome 21. These individuals share common features, but there are also great variations in abilities. Some pupils with Down's have severe learning disabilities and no language, while others will be able to read and write and will go on to have jobs within the community. As a TA supporting pupils with this condition you will notice that many will have speech difficulties, specifically problems with pronunciation. Individuals with Down's will often have difficulties hearing. In addition there can be problems with fine and gross motor skills. The most limiting problem in the past has been low expectations.

Set high but realistic expectations

Often pupils live up to or in some cases live down to expectations. Set the pupils you support high but realistic expectations. Pupils with Down's may like you to sit next to them all the time. But as a TA you need to balance their requests with the realisation that you need to treat them as you would any other pupil in the class. Doing everything for a pupil with Down's is not teaching them how to be an independent learner. Pupils need to be taught how to solve their own problems, so if a pupil cannot spell a word, rather than depending on you to spell it for them they need to know how to go about finding the correct spelling. This may be found in a dictionary or it may be in the text that they are reading. As such pupils need to learn the skills necessary to become independent learners, be there for them but also encourage them to work it out for themselves. However, saying that, the set tasks need to be realistic, i.e. achievable.

Be aware of who Down's syndrome pupils are sitting with. Ideally they should be placed next to pupils who are supportive and who will be good role models. If you realise that this is not the case you need to discuss your observations with the teacher.

Do not accept immature or silly behaviour as being part of the condition of Down's. Remember, pupils will live up or down to your expectations.

Be aware of limitations in hearing

Pupils with Down's syndrome will often have problems with hearing (see pages 100–101). If the pupil is to listen to the teacher it is important that the pupil is placed near the front of the class. If possible, background noise should be kept to a minimum as this will help the pupil to listen. If working one-to-one with a pupil or in a small group a TA needs to think carefully regarding the location. Having a one-to-one session in a busy part of the library would not be a good idea. When speaking to a pupil it is important that the teacher and TA face the pupil, maintain eye contact and speak clearly and simply. It is helpful to use visual cues such as pictures, facial expressions and body language to support your communication. Pupil's with Down's syndrome are very good at learning from visual cues.

Be aware of limitations in memory and work towards improving memory skills

Pupils with Down's syndrome will have limited auditory memory, meaning that they will have difficulties remembering what has been said to them. Before actually speaking, it is important to get their attention by calling their name. Keep instructions short and simple. For example, 'Let's go read' is preferable to 'Come on, let's go over to the reading corner and have a look at your book.'

Sometimes individuals with Down's will repeat back to you the last part of what you said. For example, if you were to say 'You need to do questions one to five in order to finish your maths assignment', a pupil might respond 'Finish maths assignment'. From this response you might think that they have understood the task, but they might have missed the point of what questions they need to do. Always check for understanding.

As pupils with Down's will have problems with memory you might need to remind them constantly of class rules. Memory skills, such as verbal rehearsal, i.e. repeating over and over to themselves what they need to remember, can be taught. Memory games are a fun way of improving memory. Talk to your teacher or SENCO about possible games.

Encourage language development

Language, in particular pronunciation, can be difficult. A TA to begin with will need to listen very carefully to what the pupil is saying. A speech therapist will often offer advice to the school. A pupil with Down's syndrome will need to practise their language skills. A TA can help by asking the pupil open questions. Open questions such as 'What did you do last night?' encourage the pupil to expand on their use of language. Open questions are preferable to closed questions, which require a simple yes or no reply. It is important to give the pupil time to reply to your questions. Allow at least 30 seconds before attempting to rephrase the question. New terms in language are best learnt within real situations: that is, specialist terms regarding plants and trees are learnt best by looking at real plants or trees. Where this is not possible pictures should be used.

Support age-appropriate friendships

Encouraging friendships is important. Friendships are key to emotional growth, happiness and the learning of age-appropriate social skills. TAs should encourage a pupil to work and play with others. A pupil with Down's syndrome might want to hold your hand if you are supervising at break, but it might be better if they were encouraged to play with children within their year group. Special schemes such as buddy schemes or Circle of Friends (see pages 70, 87) may be helpful.

Prepare differentiated material

Pupils with Down's syndrome will often need work that is differentiated, i.e. adapted for their level of ability. While most often this will be the role of the teacher, there might be occasions when this work falls to the TA.

The advice given is to use plenty of visual cues, namely pictures and diagrams. In using pictures make sure that they are clearly related to the key words or terms that you are trying to introduce. Typed work is often more easily understood than handwriting. Worksheets should not have too much information, be it text or pictures, as this might prove over-whelming.

Dyscalculia

This term refers to individuals who have consistent problems in learning maths (see page 62). Such individuals would find the logic and language of maths difficult to understand. These individuals might find it impossible to learn their times tables. There could be difficulties in reading time, remembering the steps necessary to solve a problem and in generalising mathematical skills learnt in the classroom to real-life events.

Determining what a pupil does understand is essential

The first step in helping a pupil who is having difficulties with maths is to determine what they do understand. This is especially important as maths is taught sequentially; that is, in a step-by-step fashion with new information building on previously learnt information. As a TA you will need to talk to the teacher regarding the level the pupil is working at. The teacher might discuss the pupil's test results or mention specific targets they are working on. However, much information can be gathered through observation. When a pupil is having difficulties with a problem it is helpful to carry out a **task analysis**. A task analysis refers to the identification of the skills necessary to solve a particular task. For example, what skills are necessary in order to solve a simple addition problem? In this example a pupil would need to be able to recognise numbers, be able to count on and be able to understand the concept of addition.

Conducting a task analysis can help you, the TA, in trying to understand why a pupil has made a mistake. For example, if a pupil says that 2 + 2 = 5, is it a careless error *or* is it due to the pupil not being able to count on? As a TA you will need to use questioning techniques to establish what they do understand and why they think that 2 + 2 = 5. Once a reason has been found for the pupils' difficulty in understanding, then this information can be used to plan future work with the pupils. Your observation in this regard will be invaluable to the teacher.

Make tasks achievable

Tasks set for the pupil need to be achievable. Many a pupil, and adult for that matter, gives up on maths *not* because they lack the ability but because they have come to believe that they just cannot do it (see pages 61, 99). Such pupils need much praise and encouragement.

Constant revision is necessary

Sometimes you will find that the pupil seems to understand the problem in class but the next day they will tell you that they couldn't complete the homework because they had forgotten how to do the task. It is possible that pupils are having difficulties in internalising this information, or storing it in their long-term memory. In such cases you will need to revise constantly, or refer back to previously taught concepts. One idea that is helpful is to have the pupil write down step-by-step instructions on how to solve a particular problem. Have the pupils read these steps to you. Make sure that they understand. Pupils can use this written information to jog their memory.

Use multi-sensory techniques, but make sure they are age appropriate

Pupils who have difficulties in understanding maths will often benefit from multi-sensory techniques. Some pupils will have difficulties in thinking about maths abstractly in their head and will benefit from having hands-on materials (concrete apparatus), e.g. counters that they can operate and see. Maths games, number lines, plastic money, multi-link are very popular in primary schools but can be useful in secondary schools where pupils are still having difficulties. However, it is important that these maths games are age appropriate and that the secondary pupil does not feel that these resources are babyish. Sometimes it is helpful when presented with a problem to try to visualise it and to try and draw a picture of what the pupil understands of the problem. Often times tables can be learnt effectively through the use of music and rhyme.

Teach checking strategies

Often pupils with difficulties in maths will make careless mistakes. Again it is important to try and determine why the pupil is making these mistakes. Is it because of impulsive learning styles (see page 33), or is it because they have ineffective checking strategies? Telling pupils to check their work is not enough. Pupils need to be taught specific strategies.

Pay attention to how the work is to be presented

Attention needs to be given to the presentation format of worksheets. Too much information on a page can be seen as overwhelming. Some pupils will benefit from having lines or using graph paper as this will encourage them to write their numbers in an ordered fashion (see page 64). For younger pupils, particular areas of interest (e.g. trains, lawn mowers) can be incorporated into worksheets. Older pupils will often ask, 'Why do I have to learn this?' Such pupils will benefit from discussing how this information can be used practically in everyday life.

Dyslexia

One formal definition states that 'dyslexia is a combination of abilities and difficulties that affect the learning process in one or more of reading, spelling and writing' (The British Dyslexia Association, 2005). As a TA what you might notice is that a seemingly bright pupil is having unexpected difficulties with reading and spelling. Specifically you might notice that the pupil seems unable to sound a word out, i.e. use a phonetic approach to spelling. The pupil's work might contain bizarre spellings. You might notice that the pupil has difficulty in sequencing. Sequencing refers to placing things in the correct order. In the classroom you might notice the pupil writing letters back to front, and in spelling words the pupil might have the correct letters but place them in the incorrect order. Again sequencing difficulties might be apparent in sentence construction where the pupil writes words in the wrong order. In addition, the pupil might have difficulties remembering the days of the week or the months of the year. Sometimes pupils will have problems with visual perception (see page 52). They might report that the letters seem to move and jump around the page. Individuals with dyslexia will have a limited short-term memory; that is, they will have difficulties remembering what you have just told them. In addition, some pupils might have problems with fine and gross motor skills (see pages 89–91) or problems with hyperactivity (see pages 81–4).

Find out as much as possible about specialised programmes

Talk to the teacher or SENCO regarding advice and special programmes. There are many packages, programmes and games now available to help those who have difficulties with spelling and reading. With pupils who have difficulty with letters moving and jumping around, coloured overlays can be helpful. Some programmes work on developing skills that the pupils find difficult, e.g. spelling using a phonetic approach. Some programmes use the pupil's strengths to compensate for their difficulties. For example if the pupil has a very good memory, then they can learn memory techniques or sayings that will help them remember how to spell specific words. Often the word 'said' is remembered by phrases such as 'Sister Alice is dizzy' (see page 56). As a TA you can help pupils to create their own memory aids. The Internet is also a valuable resource for looking up tips for teaching (see page 124).

Pay attention to what the pupils achieve and to their errors

When working with pupils pay particular attention to words they have read or spelt correctly as well as words they have read and spelt incorrectly. This technique, of specifically recording their efforts in reading and spelling, is called miscue analysis (see page 49). Such careful recording can reveal patterns behind the pupils' errors. Your feedback to the teacher is vital and needs to be as specific as possible.

Praise

Pupils with dyslexia need praise. These pupils are only too well aware that reading and spelling comes easy to many of their fellow pupils. As a TA it is important to acknowledge how difficult these skills are and to praise and celebrate both effort and achievements. It is also important to stress that everyone is intelligent but that we are intelligent and learn in different ways.

Use multi-sensory techniques

Multi-sensory techniques are often used with the teaching of reading and spelling. These techniques involve implementing teaching strategies that make use of the senses of sight (visual), hearing (auditory) and touch (kinaesthetic). As stated previously, individuals will have preferences regarding whether they are visual, auditory or kinaesthetic learners.

In terms of visual learning, the pupil is presented with the written word and possibly a picture that would act as a reminder for the word. Assisting the pupil to make personalised flashcards where the word is accompanied by a picture that has personal meaning, e.g. 'L stands for lawn mower', can be useful. Sometimes pupils are asked to look in a mirror while they are making certain sounds. Therefore not only do they hear (auditory) what they are saying, but also they can see how different lip and tongue movements correspond to different sounds. This may be helpful for pupils who find it difficult to hear the difference between sounds such as 'b' and 'd'.

Pupils can be encouraged to name each letter out loud as they spell the word. This approach can reinforce learning. Having the pupils make a tape recording of themselves reading and spelling words can be useful in learning the correct spellings. This strategy is suitable for the auditory learner. The pupil presses *play* to hear the correct word, presses *pause* while they write the word and then presses *play* to hear themselves spell the word correctly. Some software packages allow for phonemes, words and whole sentences to be spoken through the computer as the pupil types in the information.

For a kinaesthetic learner hands-on involvement is important. Sometimes pupils are encouraged to trace the letters in sand, in the air or on someone's back. This teaching strategy helps them to remember hand movements that correspond to each letter. For further information refer to Chapter 4.

Epilepsy

Epilepsy refers to seizures (see page 15). Seizures are the result of disturbances in the activity of nerve cells within the brain. One type of epilepsy involves what is called a tonic–clonic seizure. This type of seizure in the past was referred to as grand mal. During this type of seizure the individual loses consciousness and falls to the ground. The body stiffens (tonic phase) and then convulses (clonic phase). Another type of seizure involves the individual going off into a trance-like state, which can last for a few seconds. This type of seizure in the past was referred to as petit mal.

If a pupil you support has epilepsy find out information regarding the type of epilepsy, the medication they are on, any side effects of medication and the necessary steps to take if they have a seizure.

Fears and phobias

Be supportive

Many individuals will have fears. However, phobias can be defined as specific intense fears that interfere with an individual's quality of life. (See also **obsessive compulsive disorder (OCD)**, page 121.)

In relation to school, some pupils may have specific fears that can at times interfere with their learning. Pupils may have a specific fear, for example, of being in a maths class (see pages 61, 95). They might even have what is known as a school phobia, an intense fear of being in school. School phobias or school refusal, i.e. refusal to attend school, can have many reasons. Possibly it could be due to what is happening in the school. The pupil may be being bullied. It is also possible that school refusal may be the result of a fear of leaving home.

SENCOs, EPs and **Educational Welfare Officers** will often be able to offer advice on how best to support the pupil.

One explanation of fears and phobias has it that they are 'conditioned emotional responses'. Conditioned emotional responses often begin with one traumatic event. One adult reported that their fear of being in a maths class could be traced back to an incident in a Year 2 class. The pupil in question reported that they made a mistake in reciting their times table and the punishment for this was to stand at the back of the class in the corner. The pupil was so upset that they wet themselves. This added further to the humiliation as the teacher then told them off in front of the class for being such a baby. From that time on, the pupil felt anxious and upset whenever they thought about maths or had to enter a maths classroom, and then did everything in their power to avoid being in a maths lesson. Needless to say that pupil never succeeded at maths.

Though this example is dramatic and one would hope that such incidents do not happen today, what this example shows is that emotions can influence the learning process. As a TA one aspect of your role is to support pupils, to listen to their worries and concerns and to try to make learning experiences positive.

A natural reaction to an intense fear (be it a fear of school, a fear of maths or a fear of leaving home) is to avoid the situation that makes one feel fearful. However, to overcome the fear, one must confront it. The pupil needs to attend school. The pupil needs to attend the maths class. The pupil needs to leave home. The pupil will need much support and encouragement to do this. It is hoped that through support the pupil in time will come to enjoy the activities that they once feared.

When psychologists treat phobias they often use a technique called 'systematic desensitisation'. Systematic desensitisation involves teaching an individual relaxation techniques and then gradually over time encouraging the individual to use these relaxation techniques as they confront their fears. The rationale behind this treatment is that the individual cannot feel relaxed and terrified at the same time.

Hearing impairments

The first point to consider is that pupils with hearing impairments (see page 34) will differ greatly in regard to how much they can hear. Some may have **conductive deafness**, others **sensori-neural deafness**.

For those pupils who have difficulties in hearing there are a number of options available. Traditional hearing aids, or radio aids, which have been likened to amplifiers, can be used. Cochlea implants involve sending electrical signals directly to the auditory nerve to provide a sensation of hearing. In addition, hearing-impaired pupils are encouraged to use lip-reading, and sign language to aid their communication.

Look out for indicators of hearing difficulties

TAs can look out for indicators that a pupil is having difficulties hearing. Such pupils may have delayed speech. Their speech may be unclear and their pronunciation difficult to understand. They may talk too loudly or too softly. It goes without saying that a child who finds it difficult to hear will have difficulties in learning to talk. If the pupil has mild hearing loss then they may not hear all of what you have said. Such pupils may constantly ask you to repeat yourself. They might fail to follow instructions, spend time daydreaming, continue with an activity after everyone else has stopped and watch others in order to discover what they have to do. Sometimes individuals might have a partial hearing loss where they can hear sounds at some frequencies but not at others. For example, a pupil might be able to hear a woman's voice but not a man's voice. If you notice any of these indicators you will need to express your concerns to the teacher.

Try to improve listening conditions

Be aware of the environment in which you and the pupil are working. Ask the pupil what helps them. Avoid very noisy environments. Try to sit near the pupil with the pupil facing you. Speak clearly and naturally and at a normal rate. Use facial expressions and gestures to aid communication. Always look at the pupil when you are talking. This might seem an obvious point, but often we continue to talk as we look down at the textbook or as we turn around and write something on the board. This is fine for most pupils, but difficult for pupils who have hearing impairments and especially difficult for pupils who rely on lip-reading.

If you are working with a pupil within a group it is important to try to manage a productive working environment. If other pupils are chatting while you are talking this will not help the hearing-impaired pupil. Encourage all the pupils to take turns and to listen to each other's contribution. If the pupil you are supporting is relying on lip-reading to help assist their hearing then you might need to repeat and paraphrase other pupils' contributions. Make other pupils aware of what would help the hearing-impaired pupil. Always check with the pupil to ensure that they have understood what has been said.

Set achievable tasks

Set tasks that are realistic and achievable. Asking a hearing-impaired child to watch a video and take notes while doing so is impossible. As a TA you might offer to take the notes yourself while the pupil watches. Trying to cope and hear in a mainstream class will be extremely tiring for a hearing-impaired pupil. As you get to know the pupil you support you will be able to pick up on signs that they are getting tired. Possibly you will need to work in short bursts and take breaks.

Muscular dystrophy

There are many types of muscular dystrophy and related neuromuscular conditions. Most of these conditions are inherited. They are characterised by ongoing or progressive loss of muscle strength as muscle wasting or nerve deterioration occurs. They can shorten life expectancy and at present there are no cures. Pupils with these conditions can be in mainstream or special schools (Muscular Dystrophy Campaign, 2001).

Seek advice

A physiotherapist can offer the school valuable advice on the types of activities or active exercise that will delay the deterioration in muscle strength. Though exercise is needed, care must be taken that the pupil does not become over-tired in the process.

As a TA you may be involved with these exercise programmes. Good posture and good seating are essential. Advice needs to be taken on suitable angled writing surfaces, pens and pencils that will maximise good posture.

As the pupil will tire easily, consideration needs to be given to spreading out activities. Keyboard skills need to be introduced and taught before the ability to write requires too much effort.

Be aware of mobility issues

At an early stage the pupil will not need a wheelchair but will suffer from what is known as an unsteady gait; that is, they could fall frequently and have problems in getting themselves up. Consideration needs to be given to the pupil's timetable to limit the need to move between rooms and to avoid areas that need to be approached by steps or stairs. If the pupil needs to move to a different room, allowing the pupil to leave early so as to avoid busy corridors is helpful.

It is important not to single children out as different from their peers. For example, on a school visit to a nature reserve it would not be appropriate to say to the class: 'We can't go this way because David is in a wheelchair.' In planning school visits it is necessary to plan and discuss with the teacher any potential obstacles to the pupil's mobility. This discussion needs to take place before the visit.

Involve pupils in activities

A pupil with physical disabilities will need to be able to access all areas of the school. Consideration needs to be given as to how to involve a pupil in activities. In PE, a pupil who cannot run and kick a ball can be involved in the game by keeping score or acting as the referee. Those pupils who have problems with balance might at times need to hold onto someone for support. If a child is in a wheelchair and you need to assist them at break time, let the child take the lead and tell you where they want to be pushed rather than you pushing them where you think they want to go.

Post-traumatic stress disorder

Post-traumatic stress disorder (PTSD) details the negative reactions of an individual to a traumatic event. The traumatic event could involve being a survivor of a natural disaster such as a flood or fire, it could involve witnessing the death of a loved one, being the victim of rape or torture or witnessing domestic abuse. The negative reactions or symptoms of PTSD could include having flashbacks, nightmares and anxiety attacks, feeling depressed or suicidal, feeling no emotion and being detached and unresponsive to others. While adults suffer from PTSD so do children, though depending on the age of the child the symptoms of PTSD can vary from that of an adult sufferer. Very young children may have trouble sleeping, they may develop a fear of strangers and a fear of being separated from the main carer. It is thought that a teenager suffering from PTSD will display symptoms very similar to that of an adult sufferer.

A school will need to look out for indicators of PTSD. Children who came to this country as refugees may be particularly vulnerable, as they may have lived through war and seen family members killed (see pages 46, 74).

Professional advice needs to be sought.

Self-mutilation and self-harm

If a pupil wishes to talk to you regarding their behaviour listen to what they have to say. Separate the behaviour from the person. Be honest and say that their behaviour upsets you but that you understand that it helps them to cope. Listen to them and respect their feelings. Don't be critical or blame them for their behaviour (Young People and Self Harm, 2004).

Above all, report all disclosures to the teacher or relevant member of staff and seek professional advice (see pages 16, 68, 69, 88).

Sexually inappropriate behaviour

Refer all incidents to the teacher or other members of staff

Indicators to look out for would be masturbation, exposure of genitalia or flashing, sexually explicit language, drawings reflecting sexually explicit acts and sexually explicit role-play that involves other pupils. There could be a number of explanations behind this inappropriate behaviour. Some individuals, especially those with more extensive learning disabilities, may masturbate in public. These individuals will need to be taught that this activity needs to be conducted in a private place and that a classroom or the school hall is not appropriate. Some pupils may use sexually explicit language, or describe acts that they have seen or watched on videos. Sadly, sexually inappropriate behaviour for some children will be an indicator that they themselves have been the victims of sexual abuse. Tragically one way for a child to cope with sexual abuse is to re-enact this abuse on someone else. If you observe any sexually inappropriate behaviour this will need to be communicated to the teacher. In some cases the pupil displaying such behaviour, and any other children that have been affected, will need professional support.

Speech difficulties

In discussing speech difficulties it is first important to distinguish between *expressive* and *receptive* language and between a language *delay* and a language *disorder*. Expressive language describes how an individual communicates; this includes speech production, vocabulary and grammar. Receptive language details the extent to which an individual understands what is being said to them. A language delay is when a child progresses in their speech development in the normal way, but at a slower rate to most others. A language disorder is when that development does not follow the normal pattern and is erratic in its progress.

The role of the speech therapist

One of the most common speech impairments a TA will encounter in the classroom is problems with articulation; that is, problems in pronouncing words and sounds correctly. Often these problems are minor, e.g. a young child who says 'wee-waw' for 'see-saw' or 'nana' for 'banana'. The school will often receive advice from the speech therapist on specific programmes that the pupil will need to practise in order to correct their pronunciation. The pupil will need to work at these exercises and it is often the TA who will be called upon to assist the pupil in these exercises.

What to do if you just don't understand what the pupil is trying to say

Often what a TA and teacher will find extremely difficult is how to respond to the child whom they cannot understand. This becomes more difficult when it is obvious that the child is trying very hard and clearly frustrated at not being able to make themselves understood. The worse thing to do in this incident is to pretend that you do understand. It is best to be honest and say to the pupil, 'I know you are trying really hard, but I don't understand'. Sometimes you can then ask the pupil to show you, act it out, draw a picture or sometimes you can ask another pupil if they know what this pupil is trying to say. The important part is that you praise the pupil's efforts for communication and make it clear that they are getting better at expressing themselves. A pupil with severe difficulties in articulation may be taught an augmented or additional method of communication, such as British Sign Language or Makaton.

To help you understand the pupil's attempts to communicate it is helpful to have a conversation with them regarding a very specific area, e.g. a book that they are reading. Point to individual pictures. Point to specific words or numbers and ask the pupil to pronounce them. This will give you an insight into how the pupil is trying to communicate these concepts.

Supporting a pupil who stammers

As a TA you might support a pupil who stammers. Stammering refers to speech that is hesitant, jerky and tense. Some pupils with stammers will get stuck on certain words, so much so that no sound actually comes out or only a strangled sound. Often in stammering, sounds are prolonged, e.g. 'Wwwwweeee', or there are repetitions of part of a word, e.g. 'Do-do-do-don't do that.'

Understandably a pupil who stammers may show signs of nervousness and anxiety in situations where they have to speak. As a TA you can support such a pupil by asking them first what you can do to make it easier for them. When they are speaking it is important to maintain eye contact, let them talk at their own pace, do not hurry or rush them, listen to what is being said and give them lots of praise for their efforts.

In working with pupils who stammer, consideration needs to be given to other pupils they sit with or other pupils they are required to work with. A pupil who stammers needs to work with other pupils who are supportive. Your feedback to the teacher regarding who the pupil would find supportive would be very useful.

Adapt your language to the pupil

Sometimes pupils with difficulties in understanding verbal language are very good at picking up non-verbal cues. You might therefore make mistakes in over-estimating the comprehension levels of certain pupils. A speech therapist's advice is useful in that they can determine through testing how many key words within a sentence the pupil understands. Once you have this information you can adapt your language to the pupil. If a pupil understands only one or two key words in a sentence then as a TA you need to keep your comments and instructions short and to the point.

Visual impairments

In terms of vision, pupils will vary in regard to how much they can see (see page 34). Some pupils have partial sight due to squints, cataracts, glaucoma or light-sensitivity or to particular conditions such as **Batten's disease**. Others may be so extremely long-sighted or short-sighted that, depending on the situation, they, too, are partially sighted. A pupil with no sight will need to be taught alternative methods of reading, most commonly *Braille* or *Moon*. Braille is a tactile system of communication consisting of raised dots that correspond to letters of the alphabet. Moon is a tactile system of communication based on raised letters that are very similar to the letters of the alphabet.

Those who are partially sighted will need to have adaptations made to their learning environment. Such adaptations could be as basic as making sure that all work is enlarged for them, but it may also involve the use of sloping boards on which to write or the wearing of sunglasses or hats with brims in class to protect light-sensitive eyes. Resources such as magnifiers could be used or special computer programs that enlarge text and speak it back once it is typed. Some pupils will have difficulties in recognising an object if it is presented against a complex background but will be able to recognise objects on a plain background. For some pupils coloured overlays will enhance the clarity of the work to be presented.

The most common resource to aid visual impairment is glasses, and TAs will need to ensure that pupils wear their glasses for appropriate activities. Some visually impaired pupils will benefit from adapted resources such as balls with bells inside so they can join in games or coloured pens which have a different smell for each colour. Advice will need to be sought from the LEA's specialist adviser for visual impairment and from the local mobility officer.

Sometimes the classroom environment needs to be made 'visually friendly' by having the doors painted in a contrasting colour to the wall and the door handle in a contrasting colour to that of the door. In any case, as part of a school's 'Disability Access Plan', all stairs around the school should have yellow strips placed on their treads.

Checklist

✓ Find out as much as possible about the pupils you are supporting.
✓ Have high expectations for all the pupils you work with.
✓ Encourage independence.
✓ Report worrisome behaviour.
✓ Avoid labels – see the pupil first.
✓ Encourage friendships.

8 On being a TA

Certainly not the money

Satisfaction of a job well done

There are some jobs, possibly, where you can sit for hours and be bored out of your head, yet go in day after day and quite enjoy it. There are other jobs with high levels of stress and responsibility, which could wear you down, except for the large pay cheque at the end of every month.

Being a TA is nothing like either of these. For whatever reason you do the job, it is certainly not the money.

So why do the job? Or, perhaps more pertinently, why stay in the job once the initial 'honeymoon' period is over?

For many, one reason is the hours. By restricting employment to school hours, the job can fit in with family commitments, particularly the bringing up of young children.

At a basic level, however, the reason to stay in the job surely has something to do with the satisfaction gained through doing it. Frustrations, disappointments and setbacks are there in abundance, but there is also the incredible sense of well-being and downright pleasure in seeing children who once struggled make progress. Knowing that you played a significant part in drawing a child out of their shell to participate in class discussions; recognising that a pupil is reading confidently and enjoying it because of your support; acknowledging that a pupil with challenging behaviour is still in school and is learning the values of the school because of your patient and caring approach – all these things add up to a great deal.

There is no other feeling like it. This is why you do the job.

How to buy a sense of humour

Developing a shared sense of humour

However, there are times when the job of a TA is tough. At these times, a good sense of humour, along with other mechanisms such as friendships and team spirit, is important. It is not possible, of course, to buy a sense of humour, but there are ways to develop one. The first is not to take yourself too seriously. There are very few situations where there is absolutely no funny side. This is not to say that you become flippant or irresponsible, far from it. Nor do you develop humour at the expense of anybody else, adult or child, by laughing at them. A shared sense of humour grows out of a shared professionalism, a shared sense of responsibility. It is when you know that everyone is working hard and doing a good job that you can be relaxed enough to laugh.

Why unions are important

Find out about trade union membership

Trade unions were formed to stand up for the rights of exploited workers. Whilst the plight of TAs in schools today probably does not compare with the situation of the Tolpuddle Martyrs who, early in the nineteenth century, got transported to Australia for organising a trade union, there can be a genuine sense of being underpaid and undervalued. When TAs really were mums coming in to help put up displays or tidy paint pots, perhaps the issue of pay and conditions was not so relevant. Now, however, the situation has totally changed. TAs are professionals in their own right who perform a vital role in school, and they should be recognised as such. Schools would be unable to meet what is now expected of them were it not for TAs. This has transformed the work of the TA, but it has yet to transform pay and conditions.

Several trade unions are promoting the rights of TAs, the largest being UNISON, but the Association of Teachers and Lecturers (ATL) also has a section for TAs. Trade unions give a corporate voice to people who, otherwise, would have little say. Joining a union gives more weight to that voice (see page 12).

Being part of a union is perhaps more important now for a TA than it has ever been. The national agenda of 'Workforce Remodelling' could dramatically affect the way TAs are employed and paid. As an individual TA, you will have little say in how this 'remodelling' takes shape, but as a member of a union which represents you and thousands like you, your influence grows.

'There's got to be something easier'

When things get tough – the tough find someone to talk with

There will be days which do not go well. You have a disagreement with the class teacher or the SENCO. You are verbally abused or even hit by a child. You feel you are getting nowhere with a particular pupil or group of pupils and you do not know what else you can do. You look around you and see people who *must* be doing easier jobs. The grass is always greener on the other side of the hill.

Talk to somebody. Do not suffer in silence. Most of all, do not think you are the only one feeling the way you do or, even more seriously, that there is something wrong with you for feeling frustrated or let down. One of the strengths of good schools is the friendship and support groups which develop between staff, which is why being a 'team player' is such an essential part of the job.

Throughout this book, the importance of the support provided by other TAs has been emphasised. Talk to them. You should also be able to discuss any matter of concern with the SENCO – that's what they are there for. You need a listening and sympathetic ear.

If the situation is serious, then follow the school's procedures, which may involve following the grievance policy (see page 11). The thing not to do is let off steam in an inappropriate situation or in an inappropriate way.

How to be realistic about yourself, about others and about the school

Be realistic in your expectations

Nothing and nobody is perfect. Working closely with other adults and with children, all of whom are fallible human beings, you will inevitably have bad days. If you do not, you are either incredibly lucky or you have missed the plot.

Being realistic in your expectations is vital. You should expect to be treated with respect and dignity by all in the school, adults and children alike. You should expect to be treated as a professional member of staff, equal in status if not in responsibility with teachers. But you should not expect everything to be perfect and to go smoothly or entirely to your satisfaction. You need to go into the job with your eyes open, and with rose-tinted spectacles well removed from your eyes.

Be realistic about yourself

There is an old saying which goes something like this: 'As a person thinks in his heart, so he is.' What this essentially means is that the way we think about ourselves will largely determine the way we try and live. If we feel we should be able to meet every single need which comes our way, that is what we will try and do. But, of course, this is an impossible expectation.

The first principle, therefore, about being realistic about yourself is – know yourself. Technically, this is developing 'intra-personal intelligence'. It means things like being aware of what you are good at, where your strengths lie; but it also means acknowledging your limitations. This is not to admit failure or weakness, it is simply saying that you are human and you cannot do everything.

Another principle is avoiding comparing yourself with other people, particularly other TAs. It is all too easy to feel that everyone else is coping better than you or that they are doing a better job than you. Allowing yourself to feel like this is a sure way to sink under pressure.

So, do not put yourself under unrealistic pressure.

Be realistic about others

Tragically, other people are just like us. They are all trying their best and all have areas of ability and areas where they are not so successful. Everyone gets tired and irritable, saying and doing things they later wished they hadn't. So, go into the job with the knowledge that, at some stage, you will feel misunderstood or just plain ignored. Having said that, your expectations of others should be that you will also be listened to, taken seriously and valued as a member of the team. If this is not the case, there is something wrong with the dynamics of the school.

Be realistic about the school

Schools cannot meet all the needs of every single pupil in their care. They were never designed for that. If you enter the job expecting to be able to give answers to every problem faced by the children you work with, you will be continually frustrated.

Schools cannot work miracles, but they can and do make a difference. You can't change everyone's world everywhere, but you can help change somebody's world somewhere. This is what you are doing in school.

A realistic expectation of school, therefore, is that it can make children's lives better, even if it cannot transform them. Most children's lives do not need transforming, yet some might. In your role as TA you may well find yourself becoming emotionally involved with certain children. This is not

in itself wrong, but it can be a danger. Part of developing a professional attitude is to keep a measure of distance between yourself and the child. If you
get too involved you may begin, subconsciously, to develop unrealistic
expectations of how much the school can or should affect the life of a
child. This can easily lead to feelings of frustration with other staff or with
the system if you feel that not enough is being done.

It is always worth remembering that the time children spend in school,
whilst crucial and formative, is only a fraction of their lives.

Stress management

What you can do if you feel stressed

Being a TA can be stressful. Hopefully, what has been said already will go a
long way towards managing that stress. Stress, by itself, is a good thing. It
energises and motivates us. The problems begin only when we experience
too high a level of stress.

Of course, stress can arise from any quarter. Family difficulties, illness,
loss can all contribute to high stress levels, but so can issues at work. One
key element which seems to contribute to stress is that of control. If you are
in a situation over which you feel you have little or no control, your stress
levels are likely to rise. As a TA in a busy school, this may be exactly how
you feel. You may view yourself as having a challenging job to do, but with
little control over how or when it is done. This, in itself, can be stressful. It
is even more stressful when you feel you could do your job more effectively
with some alterations to what happens, but nobody is willing to take your
suggestions onboard.

How do you manage this? In his book *The Games People Play*, Eric
Berne describes constructive human relationships in terms of people interacting as adult-to-adult (Berne, 1964). Alternative, less constructive
relationships occur when people feel inferior to or superior to others,
something he describes as parent–child relationships. One important way
you can help manage stress is to see yourself, and therefore act, as an adult
interacting with other adults. You are not inferior to anybody else, but
neither are you superior.

Another way to help manage stress is to remind yourself of the limits of
your responsibility in the school. When working a lot with individual
pupils or with small groups, it can be all too easy to begin to feel a responsibility for their education that is beyond your role. Always bear in mind
that you are not solely responsible for what happens to pupils in school. For
sure, you have a part to play, and it is an important part; but it is only a part
nevertheless.

A third way to avoid stress is to look out for hidden agendas, conscious or otherwise. Over the years as a TA you may well have developed an expertise in a particular area of education, such as dyslexia (see pages 96–8), Down's syndrome (see pages 92–4) or Asperger's syndrome (see pages 85–8). Stress can be heightened when you feel you have more knowledge than anyone else, and that your role is to bring the rest of the school up to speed. Stress can be lowered when you accept that this is not the case. It may have become your agenda, but it is not the agenda of the school as a whole.

Every member of staff, even the head teacher, needs to recognise that the school is bigger than any one person. If we all seek to pursue our own private agendas, however commendable they may be in themselves, we will experience undue stress. Stress is lessened as we contribute what we have to the larger scheme of things and let those with responsibility for managing the school as a whole decide what to do with it.

Looking after your needs as a TA

How to meet your needs

Who is going to look after your needs in school? Ultimately, you are. You are, because you alone really know what your needs are. No one else is going to be able to guess what these may be. For sure, it is the responsibility of the senior management of the school, including the SENCO, to ensure that the overall structure of the school makes for harmonious and effective relationships; and it is the responsibility of class teachers to organise their classes so that TAs are deployed well. But it is the responsibility of each member of staff, not only TAs, to speak up if things are not going as they should.

Throughout this book, emphasis has been placed on communication, and we end on the same theme. If you feel that, for whatever reason, your needs are not being looked after, talk about it. You need to speak to the class teacher, to the SENCO, to the deputy head or head. You must not suffer in silence.

As a final note, we end where we began. In the mixture of excitement, success, disappointment, frustration, fulfilment, professionalism and fallibility that is every school, as we have seen, a *problem-solving* rather than a 'problem-creating' or a 'problem-complaining' mentality is all important. So long as this is in place across the school there is little that cannot be over-come and put right.

Checklist

✓   There are many good reasons for being a TA.
✓   Tensions and pressures will arise – you need to have strategies in place to deal with them.
✓   Be realistic about yourself, about others and about the school.
✓   Managing stress is an important part of making the job enjoyable.
✓   Your needs as a TA must be met if you are to do the job properly.

Appendix

EXAMPLES OF WRITING FRAMES

Table 3.1

Fact sheet
The life cycle of a frog
1. Frogs lay eggs. This is called frog spawn. (The pupil completes the rest of the sheet)
2.
3.
4.
5.

Table 3.2 True or false? (The pupil writes a series of statements on a topic, some of which are true and the others false. Another pupil needs to write T or F beside each one.)

True	Sometimes it snows in the winter.
False	The sky is always green.

Table 3.3 Story boards can be used to help sequence stories and ideas

(a)

(Text)	Ghosts can be scary.	This ghost is friendly.
(Picture of ghost)	(The pupil draws a picture of a scary ghost)	(The pupil draws a picture of a friendly ghost)
(The pupil completes the rest of the sheet)		

(b)

(Picture of a beach)	
(Text)	Sam had always wanted to search for buried treasure. (The pupil completes the rest of the sheet)

Glossary

Active listening Communicating to the person we are talking with that we have indeed heard and understood them, accomplished by techniques such as rewording and reflecting.

Asperger's syndrome (AS) Difficulties with social communication, building and maintaining friendships and giving expression to imaginative ideas – also known as 'high functioning autism'.

Assessment for learning Assessing and marking children's work in a way which sets them targets.

Attention deficit/hyperactivity disorder (ADD/ADHD) Medical diagnoses which describe a range of emotional and/or behavioural difficulties such as extreme impulsivity, inattentiveness and continuous activity (always on the go). Evident before the age of 7 and constant in different contexts.

Auditory learners *See* Learning styles

Autism/autistic spectrum disorder (ASD) Severely impairs a person's ability to maintain normal contact with the world. Appears before the age of 3.

Batten's disease Children with this condition will have learning disabilities, worsening seizures and suffer progressive loss of motor skills, eventually becoming blind, bedridden and unable to communicate. At present this condition is not preventable and always fatal.

Brain-gym Programme of physical exercises designed to stimulate the brain, an essential aspect being access to drinking water throughout the day.

Cerebral palsy A term used to describe various disorders that affect movement. Appearing in the first years of life, it will affect individuals in different ways and may change over time. Some will have difficulties with fine motor skills, while others might have difficulties with balance, walking or involuntary movements.

Child Protection Liaison Officer (CPLO) The designated member of staff who is responsible for overseeing and administering issues relating to child protection.

Circle of Friends An approach that aims to support pupils with emotional and behavioural problems involving arranging, with permission of the young person involved, a group of friends (selected from other pupils) who will support the pupil with help and guidance from the teacher.

Conductive deafness Sounds cannot pass through the outer and middle ear to the cochlea and auditory nerve in the inner ear. Often caused by fluid in the middle ear (glue ear) which is particularly common in children under 5 and often clears up naturally, though in some circumstances this condition will require further intervention.

Constructive feedback A type of feedback where we say difficult things but in a manner that is seen as positive and helpful, acknowledging what has been accomplished and focusing on what is still needed.

Continuing professional development (CPD) The training undertaken by all members of a school staff to enhance their own professional expertise.

Differentiation A means by which teachers offer a common curriculum to all pupils in their classes, but tailored to meet the needs of individuals.

Down's syndrome A genetic condition, involving an extra chromosome.

Dyscalculia A specific learning difficulty related to maths, particularly numeracy.

Dyslexia Primarily a specific difficulty with learning to read, write and/or spell, often accompanied by poor organisational skills.

Dyspraxia (developmental coordination disorder) Impairment of the organisation of movement that is often accompanied by problems with language, perception and thought. Handwriting is often a particular difficulty, along with clumsiness. Symptoms are evident from an early age, often from birth.

Educational psychologists (EPs) Qualified teachers who have trained further in psychology. Support pupils and adults working with pupils who are experiencing sustained difficulties in learning or behaviour. Not to be confused with medical psychiatrists.

Education Welfare Officers (EWOs) LEA staff working with pupils and families who have social difficulties with school such as poor attendance.

Fragile X A chromosome disorder where one of the genes on the X chromosome is faulty. Symptoms include learning disabilities, hyperactivity, ADD, anxiety and emotional and behavioural problems. In addition there are physical characteristics of long faces, large ears, flat feet and hyper-extensible joints. Individuals with Fragile X can have normal intelligence or might have severe learning disabilities.

Grapheme Written representation of a 'unit of sound' (**phoneme**), i.e. the written alphabet.

Hand–gym Series of exercises designed to promote the development of fine motor control.

Ideal self How an individual would like to be.

Inclusion The process whereby, so far as possible and in compliance with parental preference, all pupils regardless of ability or disability are educated in their local mainstream schools.

Individual Education Plan (IEP) A tool to plan intervention for pupils with special educational needs. Sets out what should be taught which is *additional to* or *different from* what would normally be delivered in the class, focusing on three or four short-term targets which are SMART (Specific, Measurable, Attainable, Relevant and Timed).

Kinaesthetic learners *See* Learning styles.

Learning objective The focus of any one particular lesson which should be understood by all pupils and their work assessed in relation to that learning objective.

Learning styles An individual's unconscious preference in regard to how they process and learn new information. Some learn better through hearing (a**uditory learners**), others through what they see (**visual learners**) and others through what they touch or handle (**kinaesthetic learners**). Most employ a combination of all three learning styles, which is why schools seek to teach using 'VAK' (Visual, Auditory and Kinaesthetic) techniques.

Literacy Hour A core part of the **National Literacy Strategy**, it is divided into four main sections: shared text work, shared word/sentence work, guided or independent work, and the plenary session.

Looked After Children (LAC) All children and young people who are on Care Orders or who are accommodated under The Children Act (1989) or who are remanded into the care of the local authority.

Looked After Link Teacher (LALT) The designated member of staff who oversees and administers issues relating to Looked After Children.

ME (Myalgic Encephalomyelitis) Also known as *chronic fatigue syndrome* or *post-viral syndrome*. Pupils with this condition will often have prolonged absences from school and will need varying levels of academic and physical support when they return to school.

Miscue analysis A means of assessing a pupil's reading errors which enables targeted teaching to be given.

Multi-sensory Describes materials which seek to employ as many senses as possible in the learning process.

National Curriculum Sets out the minimum that has to be taught in schools, and a framework against which attainment can be measured. For each subject there are *programmes of study* which set out what pupils should be taught, and *attainment targets* which set the level of performance pupils are expected to achieve.

National Literacy Strategy (NLS) Introduced in 1998 to provide teaching plans for literacy to put the National Curriculum into practice in primary schools, it gives teaching objectives for each term.

National Numeracy Strategy (NNS) Introduced in 1999, it illustrates how maths can be taught from Reception to Year 6. 'Key objectives' are set out for each year group. The NNS established a daily 'Numeracy Hour', with an emphasis on mental maths and a variety of teaching and recording strategies.

Obsessive compulsive disorder (OCD) This can occur in children and adolescents as well as adults. Obsessions are annoying thoughts (e.g. thoughts about being contaminated) and compulsions are useless behaviours (e.g. washing hands every five minutes). When obsessions and compulsions happen over and over again to the point that they interfere with everyday life, this is OCD.

Occupational therapists (OTs) Health professionals who are involved in the assessment and treatment of disorders of movement.

Onset A term used in **phonics** – the initial consonant or consonant cluster in a word.

Phonemes The smallest unit of sound that can affect a meaning within a word.

Phonics The 'building blocks' of written language allowing the 'decoding' of written words into sounds or the construction of written sounds into words.

Phonological awareness/phonology Awareness of sounds within words, e.g. ability to generate rhyme and alliteration, or to segment and blend sounds.

Physiotherapists Health professionals who are involved in the assessment and treatment of disorders of movement.

Rime A term used in **phonics** – that part of the word containing the vowel and the final consonant or consonant cluster.

Self-esteem This involves evaluation; that is, comparing the way you are to the way you would like to be.

Self-image How an individual describes themselves.

Semantic pragmatic disorder Problems with semantics (the meaning of words) and pragmatics (the way language, both verbal and non-verbal, is used in social interactions). Individuals with ASD and Asperger's will often have semantic pragmatic language difficulties, experiencing difficulties in understanding humour, appreciating others' point of view, detecting sarcasm, reading body language or facial expressions and will have difficulties in understanding social situations.

Sensori–neural deafness The tiny hair cells in the cochlea that normally convert sound waves into electrical signals that travel to the auditory nerve in the brain are damaged or missing.

Sight vocabulary Learning words as whole units to repeat 'on sight' rather than working them out.

Sotos' syndrome A genetic condition sometimes referred to as *cerebral gigantism* – causes physical overgrowth and developmental delays in the first year of life. Children with this condition are bigger, heavier and have distinctive larger heads than their peers. In addition they might have problems with speech and motor skills which may continue into adulthood.

Special educational needs (SEN) 'A child has special educational needs if he or she has a learning difficulty which may be the result of a physical or sensory disability, an emotional or behavioural problem or developmental delay' (Education Act, 1981). 'Children have special educational needs if they have a *learning difficulty* which calls for *special educational provision* to be made for them' (Education Act, 1996, Section 312).

Special Educational Needs Code of Practice Issued by the government in November 2001, which all schools *must have regard to* in making provision for children with SEN. Its aim is to help schools, teachers and LEAs understand their responsibilities in meeting the needs of all pupils with SEN.

Special Educational Needs Coordinator (SENCO) The person or persons in school responsible for overseeing the day-to-day operation of special needs provision.

Speech and language therapists Health professionals who assess and review individual children, provide resources and give advice where there is a concern over language.

Statements of educational need Documents regulated by law setting out the educational and non-educational needs of individuals and the provision to be put in place to meet those needs.

Syllables A word or part of a word which contains one and only one vowel sound. It can be clapped as a 'beat' – one beat is one syllable.

Task analysis The identification of the skills necessary in solving a particular task.

Teaching strategy Activities that a teacher or teaching assistant use to promote learning. This could include reading textbooks, watching demonstrations, copying from the board, group work, role-play activities, having discussions, etc.

Teaching styles The ways in which an individual approaches the teaching process. Teaching styles include aspects of pupil involvement and emphasis on the importance of rules. Often an individual's teaching style is based on their preferred learning styles and their experience of teaching.

Tourette's syndrome Characterised by a combination of muscular tics (twitch-like movements) and may include vocal tics (sayings that are rude or unpleasant). These tics are distressing and obviously cause difficulties in social interactions.

Visual learners *See* Learning styles.

Visual timetable The routine of the day and/or week set out in pictures as well as words.

Williams' syndrome A chromosome disorder where there is a micro-deletion of part of chromosome 7. Individuals with this syndrome have characteristic elfin features, wide mouth and a large, slack bottom lip. Though individuals will have good articulation they often appear brighter than they are. Their ability to talk will mask certain learning difficulties.

Additional resources

Anti-Bullying Network:
http://www.antibullying.net

Chronic fatigue syndrome:
www.youngactiononline.com

Department for Education and Skills (lots of valuable information that can be ordered):
http://www.dfes.gov.uk/sen

Information on dyslexia:
www.dyslexia-inst.org.uk

Information on measuring preferred learning styles and learning strategies for different learning styles:
http://www.support4learning.com/education/lstyles.htm

'Mental Health and Growing Up' series encompass 36 fact sheets on a range of common mental health problems experienced by young people:
www.rcpsych.ac.uk

National Association of Professional Teaching Assistants, PO Box 210, Cambridge CB4 3ZW (Tel.: 01223 224930):
www.napta.org.uk

The Fragile X Society:
www.fragilex.org.uk

Website dedicated to Teaching Assistants:
www.spare-chair.com

Bibliography

Allergy UK (2003) 'Stolen Lives: The Allergy Report'. Online. Available HTTP: http://www.allergyuk.org/stolenlives.html (1 March 2005).

Alliance for Inclusive Education (AIE) (2000) *The Inclusion Assistant*, London: AIE.

Alton, S., Beadman, J., Black, B., Lorenz, S. and McKinnon, C. (2003) *Education Support Pack for Schools*, London: Down's Syndrome Association.

APA (1995) *Diagnostic and Statistical Manual of Mental Disorders*, 4th edn, Washington, DC: American Psychological Association.

Asthma UK (2002), 'School Pack' Online. Available HTTP: http://www.asthma.org.uk/about/resource07.php (1 March 2005).

Balshaw, M. (1991) *Help in the Classroom*, London: David Fulton.

Balshaw, M and Farrell, P. (2002) *Teaching Assistants – Practical Strategies for Effective Classroom Support*, London: David Fulton.

Barkley, R. A. (1998) 'Attention Deficit Hyperactivity Disorder', *Scientific American*, September, 44–49.

Bentham, S. (2004) *A Teaching Assistant's Guide to Child Development and Psychology in the Classroom*, London: Routledge.

Berne, E. (1964/1968) *Games People Play*, Harmondsworth: Penguin Books.

Booth, T., Ainscow, M., Black-Hawkins, K., Vaughan, M. and Shaw, L. (2000) *Index for Inclusion*, Bristol: CSIE (Centre for Studies on Inclusive Education).

British Stammering Association (1997) *A Chance to Speak: Helping a Pupil who Stammers: A Practical Guide for Teachers*, London: BSA.

Brown, G. and Wragg, E. C. (1993) *Questioning*, London: Routledge.

Buttriss, J. and Callander, A. (2003) *A-Z of Special Needs* London: pfp publishing.

Buzan, B. and Buzan, T. (1993) *The Mind Map Book*, London: BBC Worldwide.

Buzan, T. (2003) *Mind Maps for Kids*, London: Thorsons (HarperCollins).

Canfield, J. (1994) *100 Ways to Enhance Self-concept in the Classroom: A Handbook for Teachers*, 2nd edn, Boston, MA: Allyn and Bacon.

Clayton, P. (2003) *How to develop numeracy in children with dyslexia*, Wisbech: LDA.

Colby, J. (2001) 'Must try harder', *Special Children*, 141(October): 34–35.

Corbett, J. (1995) *Bad Mouthing: the Language of Special Needs*, London: Cassell.

Corbett, J. (2001) *Supporting Inclusive Education*, London: Routledge/Falmer.

Cowdery, L., Montgomery, D., Morse, P. and Prince, M. (1983–1985) *Teaching Reading Through Spelling*, Wrexham: TRTS Publishing.

Dennison, P. and Dennison, G. (1989) *Brain Gym*, Ventura, CA: Edu-Kinesthetics Inc. (Available in the UK from Body Balance Books, Educational Kinesiology Foundation, London).

Department for Education (1994) *Code of Practice on the Identification and Assessment of Special Educational Needs*, London: HMSO.

Department for Education and Employment (DfEE) (2000) *Working with Teaching Assistants: A Good Practice Guide*, London, DfEE Publications.

Department for Education and Employment (DfEE) (2001) *Special Educational Needs Code of Practice*, London, HMSO.

Derrington, C. and Groom, B. (2004) *A Team Approach to Behaviour Management*, London: Paul Chapman.

Diabetes UK (2003) 'Diabetes in schools'. Online. Available HTTP: http://www.diabetes.org.uk/teenzone/school.htm (1 March 2005).

Dunn, R. and Dunn, K. (1993a) *Teaching Elementary Students through their Individual Learning Styles: Practical Approaches for Grades 3–6*, Boston, MA: Allyn and Bacon.

Dunn, R. and Dunn, K. (1993b) *Teaching Secondary Students through their Individual Learning Styles: Practical Approaches for Grades 7–12*, Boston, MA: Allyn and Bacon.

Dyslexia in the Primary Classroom (1997) Teaching Today Series, London: BBC Education in association with The British Dyslexia Association.

Dyson, A. and Millward, A. (eds) (1995) *Towards Inclusive Schools?*, London: David Fulton.

Epilepsy Scotland (2003) 'Guidelines for Teachers'. Online. Available HTTP: http://www.epilepsyscotland.org.uk/teach_guide_2.htm (1 March 2005).

EpiPen.com (2005) 'Causes of Anaphylaxis'. Online. Available HTTP: http://www.epipen.com/causes_food.aspx (1 March 2005).

Farrell, P., Balshaw, M. and Polat, F. (1999) *The Management, Role and Training of Learning Support Assistants*, London: DfEE.

Fox, G. (2003) *A Handbook for Learning Support Assistants*, 2nd edn, London: David Fulton.

Hardwick, J. (1996) 'Irregular little beasties', *Special Children*, 94 (June–July), 7–10.

Henderson, S., Markee, A., Scheib, B. and Taylor, J. (1999) *Tools of the Trade*, London: The Handwriting Interest Group, Columns Design.

Hornsby, B. and Shear, F. (1993) *Alpha to Omega*, 4th edn, Oxford: Heinemann.

Jerwood, L. (1999) 'Using special needs assistants effectively', *British Journal of Special Education*, 26(3): 127–129.

Lacey, P. (2001) 'The Role of Learning Support Assistants in the Inclusive Learning of Pupils with Severe and Profound Learning Difficulties', *Educational Review*, 53(2): 157–167.

Lewis, A. (1995a) *Children's Understanding of Disability*, London: Routledge.

Lewis, A. (1995b) *Primary Special Needs and The National Curriculum*, London: Routledge.

Lorenz, S. (1998) *Children with Down's Syndrome*, London: David Fulton.

Lorenz, S. (1999) *Effective In-class Support*, London: David Fulton.

Lorenz, S. (2002) *First Steps in Inclusion*, London: David Fulton.

Mortimer, H. (2000) *Developing Individual Behaviour Plans in Early Years*, Tamworth: NASEN.

Moyles, J. with Suschitzky, W. (1997) *'Jills of All Trades?...'* Classroom Assistants in *KS1 Classes*, London: Association of Teachers and Lecturers (ATL).

Muscular Dystrophy Campaign (2001) 'Introduction to neuromuscular conditions'. Online. Available HTTP: http://www.muscular-dystrophy.org (5 January 2005).

Nance-Dewar, S. (2002) 'Handle with Care', *Special Children*, 144(February): 28–30.

National Deaf Children's Society (2001) *Understanding Deafness*, London: NDCS Publications.

Nelson-Jones, R. (1993) *Practical Counselling and Helping skills*, 3rd edn, London: Cassell.

Numicon, Unit D, Prospect House, The Hyde Business Park, Brighton BN2 4JE.

O'Brien, T. and Garner, P. (2001) *Untold Stories: Learning Support Assistants and their work*, Stoke on Trent: Trentham Books.

Ockelford, A. (1998) 'Making sense of the world', in *Approaches to Working with Children with Multiple Disabilities and a Visual Impairment*, London: on behalf of Vital by RNIB.

Pascal, L. (2002) *The Dyslexic in the Classroom: Special Needs*, London: Publishers' Association.

Portsmouth City Council (2003) *A-Z Directory of Information Relating to the Education of Looked After Children and Young People*, Portsmouth: Portsmouth City Council.

Poustie, J. (2000) *Mathematical Solutions: An Introduction to Dyscalculia*, Taunton: Next Generation.

Rose, R. (2000) 'Using classroom support in a primary school', *British Journal of Special Education*, 27(4): 191–196.

Rose, R. (2001) 'Primary School Teacher Perceptions of the Conditions Required to Include Pupils with Special Educational Needs', *Educational Review*, 53(2): 147–156.

Royal College of Psychiatrists (2005a) 'Children who do not go out', *Mental Health and Growing up Factsheet 9*, London: Royal College of Psychiatrists.

Royal College of Psychiatrists (2005b) 'Depression in children and young people', *Mental Health and Growing up Factsheet 34*, London: Royal College of Psychiatrists.

Shaw, L. (2001) *Learning Supporters and Inclusion*, Bristol: CSIE.

Slee, R. (ed.) (1993) *Is There a Desk With My Name On It?*, London: Falmer Press.

Special Children (2000a) 'Dyspraxia – at a glance', *Special Children*, 129(May): 22.

Special Children (2000b) 'ADHD – at a glance', *Special Children*, 130(June–July), 36.

Special Children (2000c) 'Dyslexia – at a glance', *Special Children*, 132(October): 28.

Special Children (2001a) 'Down's syndrome – at a glance', *Special Children*, 134 (January): 33.

Special Children (2001b) 'Autistic spectrum disorder – at a glance', *Special Children*, 136(March): 37.

Special Children (2002) 'Deaf friendly schools', *Special Children*, 151 November–December): 36–38.

Sullivan, K. (2000) *The Anti-Bullying Handbook*, Auckland, New Zealand: Oxford University Press.

The British Dyslexia Association (2005) 'Frequently asked questions'. Online. Available HTTP: http://www.bda-dyslexia.org.uk/main/FAQs/index.asp (24 January 2005).

Thomas, G. and Feiler, A. (eds) (1988) *Planning for Special Needs*, Oxford: Blackwell.

Thomas, G., Walker, D. and Webb, J. (1998) *The Making of the Inclusive School*, London: Routledge.

Vahid, B., Harwood, S. and Brown, S. (1998) *500 Tips for Working with Children with Special Needs*, London: Kogan Page.

Watkinson, A. (2002) 'When is a teacher not a teacher? When she is a teaching assistant', *Education 3–13*, March: 58–65.

Young People and Self Harm (2004) 'Information on Self-Harm'. Online. Available HTTP:www.selfharm.org.uk (7 January 2005).

Index

Ability grouping 30
Abuse/neglect 14, 15, 68, 88, 104, 110
Accidents 9
Active listening 25, 70
AD(H)D (Attention Deficit
    (Hyperactivity) Disorder) 34, 71, 77,
    81–4
Additional Literacy Support (ALS) 44, 51
Administration staff 1, 4, 66
Alpha to Omega 56
Analytic learners 33
Anaphylaxis/anaphylactic shock 84
Annual Reviews 20–1, 23
Apparatus/hands-on materials 32, 34–5,
    64
Appraisals 11
Asperger's syndrome 74, 86, 87, 113
Assessment 5, 7, 22, 43, 49, 55, 61, 72
Assessment for learning 22, 55
Asthma UK 85
Asylum seekers 46
Attention-seeking behaviour 70
Attention span 77
Auditory learners 32, 36, 98
Autistic Spectrum Disorder (ASD) 34,
    75, 85–8

Barkley, R. 84
Base word/ root word 55–6
Batten's Disease 106
Behaviour 16, 23, 45, 88, 92, 103, 104
Behaviour Support Plans 69
Berne, E. 112
Blends (initial consonant blends/final
    consonant blends) 52

Braille 106
Brain Gym 89
Bridge-builders 5
Bullying 14, 69, 78–9

Calculators 65
Calling out 71
Child Protection 15–6, 23
Child Protection Liaison Officer
    (CPLO) 15, 16, 69
Children Act (1989) 15
Class clown 75–6
Chromosomes 92
Circle of Friends 70, 87, 94
Coloured paper/coloured overlays 52,
    97, 106
Collaborative work 41, 54
Conditioned Emotional Responses 99
Confidentiality 23, 69, 88
Consonants 52
Constructive feedback 24
Continuing Professional Development
    (CPD) 12–13
Contracts 10–11
Copying behaviours 72–3
Counselling/pastoral support 74, 88

Defensive behaviours 73
Diabetes UK 92
Differentiation 47, 94
Digraphs (consonant digraphs/vowel
    digraphs/vowel-consonant digraphs)
    52
Disability 17
Disability Access Plan 106

Discipline 6, 7, 8
Disclosures 15–16, 68, 88, 103
Discrimination 16
Doodling 32, 35, 83
Down's syndrome 74, 92–4, 113
Duty of care 14, 88
Dyscalculia 62, 94–6
Dyslexia 52, 96–8, 113
Dyspraxia (Developmental
    Coordination Disorder) 57, 89–91

Early Identification 18
Early Literacy Support (ELS) 44, 51
Educational psychologists 18, 22, 99
Educational Welfare Officer 99
English as an Additional Language
    (EAL) 46–7, 54
Environments 33–34, 35, 47, 58, 85,
    101, 106
Epipen/Epinephine 15, 84
Expectations 7–8, 11, 30, 31, 33, 35, 41,
    67, 74, 83, 92, 110
Expressive language 104

Fight or flight 61
First Aid 1, 4
Fluency 49
Formal teaching approach 36
Further Literacy Support (FLS) 44, 51

Global learners 33
Governors 2, 12
Government 12, 16, 7, 41, 56
Grapheme 51

Hand-gym 57, 89
Handwriting 57–8, 89, 90
Head teacher 2, 3, 4, 8, 12, 20, 113
Health and safety 14–15
Hearing Impairments 34, 42, 92, 93,
    100–101
Homework 39–40, 95
Humour 31, 75, 109

ICT (information and communication
    technology) 1, 4, 47, 62, 102, 106
Ideal-self 29
Immature behaviours 73–4
Impulsive learners 33, 35, 81, 83

Inclusion 5, 16–17
Independence 5, 38–9, 41, 48, 59, 92
Individual Education Plans (IEPs) 2,
    18–19, 21, 23, 43, 69
Inhalers 85
Insecure behaviours 74–5
Insulin 91–2
Intra-personal intelligence 111
Isolated and withdrawn behaviours
    69–70, 78–9

Job descriptions 4, 5, 9
Job satisfaction 108
Job-shadowing 6

Kinaesthetic learners 32, 36, 61, 98

Labelling 30
Language delay 104
Language disorder 104
Learning difficulties/disabilities 17, 18,
    20, 23, 25, 31–32, 46, 86, 92, 104
Learning objectives 36, 55
Learning styles 31–5, 45, 77
Left-handed writers 58–9
Lip-reading 100, 101
Literacy Hour 41, 83
Local Education Authorities (LEA) 10,
    12, 17, 20, 46, 68, 106
Looked After Children (LAC) 16, 74
Looked After Link Teacher (LALT) 16
Lorenz, S. 5
Lying behaviours 78

Makaton 105
Marking 8, 22
Medication 14, 84, 85, 91, 99
Memory (auditory and/or visual) 90,
    93, 95, 97
Memory cards 64, 65
Mental health 88
Mentors/mentoring 6, 12
Mnemonics 56, 97
Miscue Analysis 49–50, 52, 97
Mind maps 44
Moon 106
Motivation 5, 37–8, 52, 53
Motor skills (gross and/or fine) 89, 97
Multi-sensory 45, 56, 62, 96, 98

'Mums' Army' 4, 6
Muscular Dystrophy Campaign 102

National Curriculum 20
National Literacy Strategy (NLS) 41, 49, 56
National Numeracy Strategy (NNS) 60
Newly Qualified Teachers (NQT) 12
Numeracy Hour 61, 83
Numicon 64
Nurse 14

Observations 43, 69, 70, 78, 92, 95
Obsessive Compulsive Disorders 99
Occupational Therapist 22
Onset 51
Overcautious/unsure behaviours 71–2, 78

Parents 8, 18, 20, 22–23, 46, 74
Pause-Prompt-Praise 48
Phonemes 50, 98
Phonics 44, 48, 49, 50, 52, 97
Phonology/phonological awareness 45, 50–51
Physiotherapists 89, 102
Planning/planning time 7–8, 18, 43, 102
Playgrounds 1, 9
Policies 4, 8, 14, 23, 85: Behaviour 66; Bulling 66, 78; Child Protection 15, 66, 68; Equal Opportunities 14, 66; Grievance 11–12, 110; Marking 22; Physical Restraint 66, 68; Race Relations 14; SEN/Inclusion 5
Praise 31, 37, 70, 71, 72, 73, 74, 75, 77, 80, 82, 89, 95, 98, 105
Prefixes/suffixes 55–6
Privacy 25–6, 27, 71
Problem solving 3, 6, 113
Professionalism 5, 6, 23, 110, 112
Programmes/intervention programmes 5, 6, 18, 21, 43, 44, 45, 60, 88, 89, 97, 104

Questioning behaviours 76–7
Questioning skills 26, 27–9, 48, 63, 72, 94

Race Relations Amendment Act (2001) 14
Reading 47–53
Receptive language 104

Record keeping 19, 21, 45
Reflecting 26, 41, 55
Reflective learners 33, 35, 77
Refugees 46, 103
Relationships with pupils 5, 24, 27, 68, 70, 79–80, 88
Relevant work 38
Repair and rebuild strategies 80
Reprographic equipment 4
Resources 1–2, 7, 18, 44, 45, 47, 52, 56, 62, 69, 96, 106
Rewards 26, 39, 66, 67, 90
Rewording 26
Rime 51
Ritalin 84

Sanctions 66, 67
School Action 18
School Action Plus 18, 22, 23
School phobia 99
Scaffolding 59
Scribing 54, 62, 73
SENCO (Special Educational Needs Coordinator) 2–4, 6, 11–13, 19, 20–1, 46, 66, 69, 78–9, 87–9, 91, 93, 97, 99, 110, 113
Seizures 15
Self-esteem 5, 28, 29–31, 70, 72, 73, 75, 78, 79, 81, 89, 90
Self-image 29
Semantic Pragmatic Disorder 86
Senior management 3, 8, 12, 23, 113
Sexual language/behaviours 15
Sight vocabulary 48–9
Signing 100, 105
Social skills 73, 74, 85–6, 94
Special Educational Needs (SEN) 2, 17–18, 46, 61
Special Educational Needs Code of Practice 2, 17–18, 22
Special Educational Needs Toolkit 17
Speech and Language Therapist 22, 86, 94, 104, 106
Spelling 55–6, 97
Springboard 60
Staff handbook 3
Stammering 105
Statements of educational need 16, 19–20, 22
Status 110

Stereotypes 30
Story Mountains 53–4
Stress/Stress management 7, 112
Student-centred approach 36
Supply teachers 8, 67
Syllables 48, 50, 51
Systematic desensitisation 100

Targets 5, 11, 18, 19, 20, 21, 22, 69, 95
Task analysis 95
Teacher-centred approach 36
Teaching Reading Through Spelling
   (TRTS) 56
Teaching strategies 18, 32, 34
Teaching styles 36–7
Team meetings 6
Teamwork 3, 10, 109, 110
Time management 37

Trades Unions 12, 109
Tripod pencil grip 58, 91

Visual Impairments 34, 42, 106
Visual learners 32, 36, 61, 93, 94, 98
Visual timetable 86–7
Volunteers 11
Vowels (long vowels/short vowels)
   51–2, 56

Wave One support 41, 42–4
Wave Two support 41–2, 44
Wave Three support 41, 44–6
Withdrawal 45, 63
Workforce Remodelling 109
Worksheets 52, 53, 94, 96
Writing 47, 53–55, 97
Writing frames 47

eBooks – at www.eBookstore.tandf.co.uk

A library at your fingertips!

eBooks are electronic versions of printed books. You can store them on your PC/laptop or browse them online.

They have advantages for anyone needing rapid access to a wide variety of published, copyright information.

eBooks can help your research by enabling you to bookmark chapters, annotate text and use instant searches to find specific words or phrases. Several eBook files would fit on even a small laptop or PDA.

NEW: Save money by eSubscribing: cheap, online access to any eBook for as long as you need it.

Annual subscription packages

We now offer special low-cost bulk subscriptions to packages of eBooks in certain subject areas. These are available to libraries or to individuals.

For more information please contact webmaster.ebooks@tandf.co.uk

We're continually developing the eBook concept, so keep up to date by visiting the website.

www.eBookstore.tandf.co.uk